Interpreting European
Financial Statements:
Towards 1992

Interpreting European Financial Statements: Towards 1992

Christopher Nobes
Deloitte Professor of Accounting
University of Reading

Butterworths
London and Edinburgh
1989

United Kingdom	Butterworth & Co (Publishers) Ltd, 88 Kingsway, LONDON WC2B 6AB and 4 Hill Street, EDINBURGH EH2 3JZ
Australia	Butterworths Pty Ltd, SYDNEY, MELBOURNE, BRISBANE, ADELAIDE, PERTH, CANBERRA and HOBART
Canada	Butterworths Canada Ltd, TORONTO and VANCOUVER
Ireland	Butterworth (Ireland) Ltd, DUBLIN
Malaysia	Malayan Law Journal Sdn Bhd, KUALA LUMPUR
New Zealand	Butterworths of New Zealand Ltd, WELLINGTON and AUCKLAND
Puerto Rico	Equity de Puerto Rico, Inc, HATO REY
Singapore	Malayan Law Journal Pty Ltd, SINGAPORE
USA	Butterworth Legal Publishers, AUSTIN, Texas; BOSTON, Massachusetts; CLEARWATER, Florida (D & S Publishers); ORFORD, New Hampshire (Equity Publishing); ST PAUL, Minnesota; and SEATTLE, Washington

A CIP Catalogue record for this book is available from the British Library.

ISBN 0 406 51170 5   1670287

Typeset by Latimer Trend & Company Ltd, Plymouth
Printed and bound in Great Britain by
Biddles Ltd, Guildford and King's Lynn

£60-00

to

Angie, Carole, Claude, Guy,
Joanna, Mark, Richard and Wyn

Preface

This book is a companion volume to *Interpreting US Financial Statements* by the same author and publisher. To some extent the structure of the two books is similar, particularly in the subject matter of Chapter 1 and in the order of material in Chapters 5 to 8. However, UK and US accounting can be seen as belonging to the same family; whereas accounting practices within Europe differ greatly. These differences are a major commercial problem, particularly for a unifying market such as the European Communities. The words 'Towards 1992' in this book's title correctly suggest the emphasis given in several parts of this book to the harmonisation process in the EC.

This book is intended primarily for such users as financial managers and auditors of multinationals and for international analysts, investors and lenders. References are kept to a minimum, given the book's largely practical rather than academic purpose. The book is designed to be useful to readers in any country, both within and without the EC. Where one European country is needed as a basis for comparison, the benchmark tends to be the UK, which is the home country of the largest number of listed companies in Europe. This benchmark will also make the book as accessible as possible to readers in North America, Australasia and the East.

In preparing this book, I have been greatly assisted by Bob Parker of Exeter University, who has made many comments on previous drafts.

The world of European accounting changes very fast, and particularly in the late 1980s and the 1990s. This book is designed to be up-to-date in late 1989, but some of its details will be overtaken by subsequent events.

Christopher Nobes
University of Reading
September 1989

Contents

CHAPTER 1

The Background to European Accounting

1.1 Introduction

The Europeanness of Accounting

Double-entry bookkeeping, listed companies, accountancy professions and published financial statements are all European inventions. The exact geography of inventions seems to be driven by commerce. For example, the increasing complexity of business in late Medieval northern Italy led to the emergence of double entry; the existence of a wealthy merchant class and the need for large investment for major projects led to public subscription of share capital in seventeenth-century Holland; the growing separation of ownership from management raised the need for audit in nineteenth-century Britain. Many countries have contributed: France led in the development of the profit and loss account; Germany gave us standardised formats for financial statements.

The Structure of the Book

The diversity of these European origins is reflected in the present differences in reporting practices in Europe. The continent is rich in the variety of its legal systems, commercial practices and ownership structures. This also contributes to the differences in accounting. A study of the background will illuminate the practical problems: and that is the subject of this first chapter.

It is increasingly the case that European companies and individuals are investing in or lending to companies in other European countries. For Britain the trend away from the Commonwealth and the USA and towards Europe has been visible since the Second World War. This trend has accelerated dramatically since entry to the European Communities (EC) and particularly as the unified market of 1992 draws closer. This means that European accounting differences have become increasingly noticeable and damaging. They militate against cross-border investment and, within multi-national companies, they hamper the appraisal of performance, the work of auditors and the movement of staff. The broad categories of difference are examined in Chapter 2.

Because of the bewildering mass of differences and the large number of countries that one could be interested in, it is useful to try to perceive a pattern in Europe. That is, it may be possible to put countries into groups by the similarity of their reporting practices. This is attempted in Chapter 3. A classification of countries can be used to impose some order on apparent chaos and to speed up the learning process: knowledge of one country can be used to draw inferences about others.

Having examined the causes and nature of differences, it is then appropriate to look at harmonisation of accounting within the EC. This was in progress throughout the 1980s, but there is still a long way to go. The basic mechanism for achieving harmonisation is change to company laws in the member states, driven by Directives which are drafted by the Commission and adopted by the Council of Ministers. These matters are the subject of Chapter 4.

The detailed differences in practice, still remaining after the harmonisation of the 1980s, are examined in Chapters 5 to 8 which deal, respectively, with presentation of accounts, asset valuation, profit measurement and group accounting. These differences are summarised in Chapter 9 which goes on to propose an international benchmark for comparison of European financial statements. Of course, language differences are also a problem, and these are addressed in a glossary at the end of the book.

There are many countries in Europe. This book will be confined to those on the western side of the Iron Curtain. Furthermore, as has been mentioned, there will be frequent reference to differences and harmonisation within the EC. Nevertheless, countries such as Sweden and Switzerland will also be mentioned from time to time. Even within the EC, there are 12 countries at the beginning of the 1990s, and it is impossible to deal with them all in detail. Illustrations tend to be drawn from major commercial countries such as France, West Germany and the Netherlands. It is also the case that discussion is generally centred around the practices of large companies.

Causes of Difference

The rest of this chapter deals with the probable causes of European differences in financial reporting. A study of this will help to set the differences into context. It will enable the reader to appreciate that the present differences are deep-seated and long-lasting.

There seems to be some consensus about which factors are involved in shaping financial reporting. Some researchers have used impressions of such causes as a means of differentiating between countries (Mueller, 1967, Part II). Other researchers have studied whether perceived differences in accounting practices correlate with such perceived causal factors (Frank, 1979). Factors which are seen as influencing accounting development include the nature of the legal system, the prevalent providers of finance, the influence of taxation, and the strength of the accountancy profession.

On a world-wide scale, factors like language or geography have been referred to by the above-mentioned researchers. To the extent that these do have some explanatory power, it seems more sensible to assume that this results from auto-correlation. That is, the fact that Australian accounting bears a marked resemblance to New Zealand accounting might be 'confirmed' by language and geographical factors. However, most of their similarities were probably not *caused* by these factors, but by their historical connection with the UK which passed on both accounting and language, and was colonising most parts of Australasia in the same period.

Further, if one wanted to encompass countries outside the developed western world, it would be necessary to include factors concerning the state of development of the economy and the nature of the political economy of the countries concerned. Of course, to some extent a precise definition of terms might make it clear that it was impossible to include some such countries. For example, if our interest is in the financial reporting practices of listed corporations, those countries with few or no such corporations have to be excluded. Fortunately, as our main purpose concerns Western Europe, there is a reasonable degree of homogeneity, in that they all have developed economies, democratic governments, listed companies, qualified account-ants, and so on. For our purposes, the following seven factors may cumulate to a powerful explanation of the cause of financial reporting differences: legal systems, providers of finance, taxation, the accountancy profession, infla-tion, theory, and accidents.

1.2 Legal Systems

Most European countries have a system of law which is based on the Roman *ius civile* as compiled by Justinian in the sixth century and developed by European universities from the twelfth century. Here rules are linked to ideas of justice and morality; they become doctrine. The word 'codified' may be associated with such a system. This difference has the important effect that company law or commercial codes need to establish rules in detail for accounting and financial reporting. For example, in the Netherlands, accounting law is contained in Book 2 of the Civil Code; in Germany and France, the Commercial Code contains accounting rules which are supple-mented by company law and, in France, by a government-controlled 'accounting plan' (see Chapter 2).

On the other hand, the UK and Ireland have a commercial legal system which has relied upon a limited amount of statute law. This is because the environment has been the 'common law' system that was formed in England primarily by post-Conquest judges acting on the king's behalf. It is less abstract than codified law; a common law rule seeks to provide an answer to a specific case rather than to formulate a general rule for the future. Although this common law system emanates from England, it may be found in similar forms in many countries influenced by England. Thus, the federal law of the USA, the laws of India, Australia, and so on are to a greater or less extent modelled on English common law. This naturally influences company law, which traditionally does not prescribe a large number of detailed, all-embracing rules to cover the behaviour of companies and how they should publish their financial statements. To a large extent, accounting within such a context is not dependent upon law. This was certainly the case in the UK until the Companies Act 1981 introduced rules from an EC Directive (see Chapter 4). Until then, the only legal instruction on matters of accounting presentation or measurement was that the accounts should 'give a true and fair view'.

This difference in legal traditions means that accounting rules tend to be law-based and slow to change in 'Roman' countries, whereas the detail is

3

Table 1.1   Some European Legal Systems

Common Law	Roman, Codified
England and Wales	France
Ireland	Italy
	W Germany
(United States)	Spain
(Canada)	Netherlands
(Australia)	
(New Zealand)	(Japan, commercial)

Note: the laws of Scotland, Israel, South Africa, Quebec, Louisiana and the Philippines embody elements of both systems.

Table 1.2   Some European Company Names

	Private	Public
Belgium	Société de personnes à responsibilité limitée (Sprl)	Société anonyme (SA)
France, Luxembourg, Switzerland	Société à responsibilité limitée (Sàrl)	Société anonyme (SA)
Italy	Società a responsibilità limitata (SRL)	Società per Azioni (SpA)
Netherlands	Besloten vennootschap (BV)	Naamloze vennootschap (NV)
Spain	Sociedad de responsibilidad limitada (SRL)	Sociedad anònima (SA)
UK, Ireland	Private limited company (Ltd)	Public limited company (PLC)
W Germany, Switzerland	Gesellschaft mit beschränkter Haftung (GmbH)	Aktiengessellschaft (AG)

controlled by accountants in 'English' countries. This affects both the nature of regulation and the nature of the detailed rules in a country.

Table 1.1 above illustrates the way in which some European countries' legal systems divide between these two types (a few other countries are included for comparison).

It will be useful at this point to discuss the nature of companies. The great bulk of business in Europe is handled by limited companies, the most common forms of which are the public company and the private company. Table 1.2 above shows the names and abbreviations of these for some European countries. The general distinction is that only for public companies is there allowed to be a market in their securities, such as a listing on a stock exchange.

Public companies are less numerous than private companies, and the laws relating to them are stricter. For example, public companies have more onerous requirements relating to minimum capital and to profit distribution. A further difference, in 'Roman law' countries is that public companies tend to have bearer shares, as opposed to registered shares. This means that there is often no share register. Public companies may then be literally anonymous (*anonyme*) or nameless (*naamloze*). (For the special features of US rules in this area, see Nobes, 1988.)

1.3 Providers of Finance

The prevalent types of business organisation and ownership also differ. In France and Italy, capital provided by the state or by banks is very significant, as are small and large family businesses. In Germany, the banks in particular are important owners of companies as well as providers of debt finance. A majority of shares in some public companies is owned or controlled as proxies by banks, particularly by the Deutsche, Dresdner and Commerz Banks. The importance of banks is increased by the prevalence of bearer shares, as mentioned above. In Germany, for example, shareholders are required to deposit their valuable bearer share certificates with their bank, which then collects dividends and exercises proxy votes. As a result of this multi-faceted influence, banks are often represented on boards of directors.

By contrast, British companies tend to be funded by share finance and to have lower gearing. Furthermore, the share finance is very widely spread, particularly compared to continental Europe. The country with the longest history of 'public' companies is the Netherlands. Although it has a fairly small Stock Exchange, shares in many large companies are widely held and actively traded.

Evidence that this characterisation is reasonable may be found by looking at the number of listed companies in various countries. Table 1.3 overleaf shows the numbers of domestic listed shares on Stock Exchanges where there are over 250 such companies. The comparison between the UK and West Germany or France is instructive. A two-group categorisation of these countries is almost as obvious as that for legal systems in Table 1.1 (taking account of size of economy and population).

Upon closer examination, the split between UK-type and continental-type is even starker. First, the continental European (and South American and Japanese) numbers are misleadingly high because of the importance of 'insider' owners, non-voting and preference shares, and cross-holdings. Secondly, the UK/US numbers need to be added to by unlisted markets and over-the-counter stocks.

Although it is to some extent the case that shares in countries like the UK (and the USA) are held by institutional investors rather than by individual shareholders, this still contrasts with state, bank or family holdings. Indeed, the increased importance of institutional investors is perhaps a reinforcement for the following hypothesis:

> in countries with a widespread ownership of companies by shareholders who do not have access to internal information there will be a pressure for disclosure, audit and 'fair' information.

Institutional investors hold larger blocks of shares and may be better

5

Table 1.3   Stock Exchanges with over 250
Domestic Companies, 1986

Exchange	Companies
American Exchange	747
Australia	1,162
Amsterdam	267
Barcelona	324
Copenhagen	274
Germany	492
Johannesburg	536
Korea	355
London	2,101
Luxembourg	253
Madrid	312
Montreal	622
New York	1,516
New Zealand	339
Osaka	1,050
Paris	482
Rio de Janeiro	658
São Paulo	592
Tel-Aviv	255
Tokyo	1,499
Toronto	1,034

Source: Fédération Internationale des Bourse de
Valuers, Annual Report.

organised than private shareholders; thus their desire for information and their command of resources should increase this pressure, although they may also be able successfully to press for more detailed information than is generally available to the public.

'Fair' was mentioned in the previous section and still needs to be defined. It is a concept related to those large number of outside owners who require unbiased information about the success of the business and its state of affairs (Stamp, 1980; Flint, 1982). Although reasonable prudence will be expected, these shareholders are interested in comparing one year with another and one company with another, thus the accruals concept and some degree of realism will be required. This entails judgment which entails experts. This expertise is also required for the checking of the financial statements by auditors. In countries like the UK and the Netherlands, over many decades this can result in a tendency to require accountants to work out their own technical rules. This is acceptable to governments because of the influence and expertise of the accountancy profession, which is usually running ahead of the interest of the government (in its capacity as shareholder, protector of public interest or collector of taxation). Thus, 'generally accepted accounting principles' control accounting. To the extent that governments intervene, they impose disclosure, filing or measurement requirements which tend to follow best practice rather than to create it.

In other European countries, banks, governments or families will nominate directors. Thus the major providers of finance have rapid access to

detailed financial information. The traditional paucity of 'outsider' shareholders has meant that external financial reporting has been largely invented
for the purposes of governments, as tax collectors or controllers of the
economy. This has not encouraged the development of flexibility, judgment,
fairness or experimentation.

As a counterpart to the above hypothesis, the following extreme idea may
be formulated:

> in countries of continental Europe where most companies are heavily influenced
> by 'insiders', there will be little pressure for published accounts or for external
> audit.

This was approximately true until the late 1980s in Europe. For example,
about a million UK companies had to publish audited accounts, whereas
only public companies (ie about 2,200 AGs) and a few other very large
companies had to do so in West Germany. Audit and publication were
extended in Germany for 1987 year-ends as a result of the EC's Fourth
Directive.

Despite this great distinction, governments in most continental countries
have recognised their responsibility to require public or listed companies to
publish audited financial statements. This happened in a 1965 Act in West
Germany; and in France and Italy the government has set up bodies
specifically to control the securities markets: in France the *Commission des
Opèrations de Bourse* (COB), and in Italy the *Commissione Nazionale per le
Società e la Borsa* (CONSOB). These bodies are to some extent modelled on
the Securities and Exchange Commission (SEC) of the USA. They have been
associated with important developments in financial reporting, generally in
the direction of Anglo-American practice. This is not surprising as these
stock exchange bodies are taking the part of private and institutional
shareholders who have, over a much longer period, helped to shape Anglo-
American accounting systems.

In France the COB was formed in 1968. Its officers are appointed by the
government. It is charged with encouraging the growth of the Bourse by
improving the quality of published information and the operations of the
market. It has established listing requirements and has investigated cases of
non-compliance with publication and disclosure requirements. Perhaps its
most obvious campaign was that to introduce consolidation. In 1968,
consolidation was extremely rare, even for listed companies. Matters
improved substantially under pressure from COB, including a requirement to
consolidate for all companies wishing to obtain a new listing. This is
discussed further in Chapter 2.

Although there are far fewer listed companies in Italy than there are in
France (Italy does not even figure in Table 1.3), the effect of the CONSOB
may be even greater than that of COB, partly because of the much less
satisfactory state of affairs in Italy before CONSOB's formation in June
1974. CONSOB has powers to call for consolidation or extra disclosures
which it has not used extensively yet. However, its real influence is linked to
the Presidential Decree No 126 of March 1975 which, after much delay, was
introduced by statutory instrument. This requires listed companies to have a
more extensive audit, undertaken by an auditing company approved by
CONSOB. This requirement is in addition to the statutory audit by *sindaci* or
state registered auditors.

1.4 Taxation

Although it is possible to make groupings of tax systems in a number of ways, only some of them are of relevance to financial reporting. For example, it is easy to divide EC countries into those using 'classical' and those using 'imputation' systems of corporation tax (Nobes and Parker, 1985, ch 15). However, this distinction does not affect financial reporting. What is much more relevant is the degree to which taxation regulations determine accounting measurements. To some extent this can be revealed in a negative way by studying the problem of deferred taxation, which is caused by timing differences between tax and accounting treatments. In the UK and the Netherlands (and the USA), for example, the problem of deferred tax has caused much controversy and a considerable amount of accounting standard documentation.

Turning to France or West Germany, it is found that the problem does not really exist to be solved; for in these latter countries it is to a large extent the case that the tax rules *are* the accounting rules. In Germany, the commercial accounts (*Handelsbilanz*) should be the same as the tax accounts (*Steuerbilanz*). There is even a word for this idea: the *Massgeblichkeitsprinzip* (the principle of bindingness).

One obvious example of the effects of this concerns depreciation. In the UK, the amount of depreciation charged in the published financial statements is determined according to custom established over the last century and influenced by the accounting standard, SSAP 12. The standard points out that:

> 'Depreciation should be allocated to accounting periods so as to charge a fair proportion of cost or valuation of the asset, to each accounting period expected to benefit from its use ... (para 3) ... Management should select the method regarded as most appropriate to the type of asset and its use in the business so as to allocate depreciation as fairly as possible. ...' (para 8).

These injunctions are of a fairly general nature, and their spirit is quite frequently ignored. Convention and pragmatism, rather than exact rules or even the spirit of the standard, also determine the method of judging the scrap value and the expected length of life.

The amount of depreciation *for tax purposes* in the UK is quite independent of these figures. It is determined by capital allowances, which are a formalised scheme of tax depreciation allowances designed to standardise the amounts allowed and to act as investment incentives. Because of the separation of the two schemes there can be a complete lack of subjectivity in tax allowances but full room for judgment in financial depreciation charges.

At the opposite extreme, in countries like West Germany, the tax regulations lay down depreciation rates to be used for particular assets. These are generally based on the expected useful lives of assets. However, in some cases, accelerated depreciation allowances are available: for example, for industries producing energy-saving or anti-pollution products or for those operating in West Berlin or other areas bordering East Germany. If these allowances are to be claimed for tax purposes (which would normally be sensible), they must be charged in the financial accounts. Thus, the charge against profit would be said by a UK accountant not to be 'fair', even though it could certainly be 'correct' or 'legal'. This influence is felt even in the details of the choice of method of depreciation, as shown by an extract from the Annual Report of AEG Telefunken:

'Plant and machinery are depreciated over a useful life of ten years on a declining balance basis; straight-line depreciation is adopted as soon as this results in a higher charge' (p 23, 1986).

A second example of the overriding effect of taxation on accounting measurement is the valuation of fixed assets in France. During the inflationary 1970s and before, French companies were allowed to revalue assets. However, this would have entailed extra taxation due to the increase in the post-revaluation balance sheet total compared to the previous year's. Consequently, except in the special case of merger by *fusion* when tax-exempt revaluation is allowed, revaluation was not practised. However, the Finance Acts of 1978 and 1979 made revaluation obligatory for listed companies and for those which solicit funds from the public; it is optional for others. The purpose was to show balance sheets more realistically. The revaluation was performed by the use of government indices relating to 31 December 1976. The credit went to an undistributable revaluation reserve. As a result of this, for depreciable assets, an amount equal to the extra depreciation due to revaluation is credited each year to profit and loss and *debited* to the revaluation account. Thus the effect of revaluation on profit (*and tax*) is neutralised. This move from no revaluations to compulsory revaluations is due to the change in tax rules. The effects spill over in the 1990s.

Somewhat similar tax-based revaluations have occurred in Italy and Spain. Further examples of the influence of tax are easy to find: bad debt provisions (determined by tax laws in many continental countries), development and maintenance expenditures (carried forward for tax purposes in Spain) or various provisions related to specific industries (see *Provisions and Reserves* in Chapter 2).

The effects of all this are to reduce the room for operation of the accruals convention (which is the driving force behind such practices as depreciation) and to reduce 'fairness'. Until the legislation following the EC's Fourth Directive, the importance of these tax effects was not disclosed in published accounts. With some variations, this *Massgeblichkeitsprinzip* operates in most continental countries except for the Netherlands. It is perhaps due partly to the persuasive influence of codification in law, and partly to the predominance of taxation as a cause of accounting.

The alternative approach is found in countries such as the UK, Ireland and the Netherlands, which have an older tradition of published accounting, where commercial rules have come first. Most of the countries on the left in Table 1.1 on p 4 above, are, in varying degrees, like this. In most cases, there is not the degree of separation between tax and financial reporting that is found in the UK in the shape of capital allowances. However, in all such countries the taxation authorities have to adjust the commercial accounts for their own purposes, after exerting only minor influences directly on them. (For details on a major US exception to this rule, see Nobes, 1988.)

1.5 The Profession

The strength, size and competence of the accountancy profession in a country may follow to a large extent from the various factors outlined above and from the type of financial reporting they have helped to produce. For example, the lack of a substantial body of private shareholders and public companies in some countries means that the need for auditors is much smaller than it is in the UK (or the USA). However, the nature of the profession also feeds back into the type of accounting that is practised and *could* be practised. For example, as has been mentioned, the 1975 Decree in Italy (not brought into effect until the 1980s) requiring listed companies to have extended audits similar to those operated in the UK could only be brought into effect initially because of the substantial presence of inter-national accounting firms. This constitutes a considerable obstacle to any attempts at significant and deep harmonisation of accounting between some countries. The need for extra auditors was a controversial issue in Germany's implementation of the EC's Fourth Directive (Nobes, 1986).

The scale of the difference is illustrated in Table 1.4 opposite, which lists the bodies whose members may audit the accounts of companies (but see below for explanation of the French and German situation). These remark-able figures need some interpretation. For example, let us more carefully compare the German to the British figures. In Germany, there is a separate, though overlapping profession of tax experts (*Steuerberater*), which is larger than the accountancy body. However, in the UK the 'accountants' figure is especially inflated by the inclusion of many who specialise in or occasionally practice in tax. Secondly, a German accountant may only be a member of the *Institut* if he is in practice, whereas at least half of the British figure represents members in commerce, industry, government, education, and so on. Thirdly, the training period is much longer in Germany than it is in the UK. It normally involves a four-year relevant degree course, six years' practical experience (four in the profession), and a professional examination consist-ing of oral and written tests plus a thesis. This tends to last until the aspiring accountant is 30 to 35 years old. Thus, many of the German 'students' would be counted as part of the qualified figure if they were in the British system. In addition, in the late 1980s, Germany resuscitated a second-tier auditing body for the audit of private companies, the *Vereidigte Buchprüfer*.

These factors help to explain the differences. However, there is still a very substantial residual difference which results from the much larger number of companies to be audited and the different process of forming a judgment on the 'fair' view.

It is interesting to note a further division along Anglo-American v Franco-German lines. In the former countries, governments or government agencies do require certain types of companies to be audited, and put certain limits on who shall be auditors, with government departments having the final say. However, in general, membership of the private professional accountancy bodies is the method of qualifying as an auditor. On the other hand, in France and West Germany, there is a dual set of accountancy bodies. Those in Table 1.4 opposite are not the bodies to which one must belong to qualify as an auditor of companies, though to a large extent the membership of these professional bodies overlaps with the auditing bodies and membership of the former enables membership of the latter. The auditing bodies are shown in Table 1.5 opposite. The professional bodies set exams, consider ethical matters, belong to the international accounting bodies, and so on. The auditing bodies are run by the state. The *Compagnie Nationale* is responsible to the Ministry of Justice; the *Wirtschaftsprüferkammer* to the Federal Minister of Economics.

Table 1.4   Public Accountancy Bodies, Age and Size

Country	Body	Founding Date*	Approx. Nos in Thousands 1987/88
United States	American Institute of Certified Public Accountants	1887	264
Canada	Canadian Institute of Chartered Accountants	1902 (1880)	44
United Kingdom	Institute of Chartered Accountants in England and Wales	1880 (1870)	85
	Institute of Chartered Accountants of Scotland	1951 (1854)	12
	Chartered Association of Certified Accountants	1939 (1891)	30
	Institute of Chartered Accountants in Ireland	1888	6
Australia	Australian Society of Accountants	1952 (1887)	55
	Institute of Chartered Accountants in Australia	1928 (1886)	17
New Zealand	New Zealand Society of Accountants	1909 (1894)	15
Netherlands	Nederlands Instituut van Registeraccountants	1895	6
France	Ordre des Experts Comptables et des Comptables Agréés	1942	11
West Germany	Institut der Wirtschaftsprüfer	1932	5
Japan	Japanese Institute of Certified Public Accountants	1948	10

*Dates of earliest predecessor bodies in brackets.

Table 1.5   Accountancy Bodies in France and W Germany

	Private Professional Body	State Auditing Body
France	Ordre des Experts Comptables	Compagnie Nationale des Commissaires aux Comptes
W Germany	Institut der Wirtschaftsprüfer	Wirtschaftsprüferkammer

1.6 Inflation

Accountants in the English-speaking world and governments in continental Europe have proved remarkably immune to inflation when it comes to decisive action. However, there are other countries where inflation has been overwhelming: in several South American countries, the most obvious feature of accounting practices is the use of methods of general price level adjustment (Tweedie and Whittington, 1984; Nobes and Parker, 1985, ch 11). The use of this comparatively simple method is probably due to the reasonable correlation of inflation with any particular specific price changes when the former is in hundreds of per cent per year; to the objective nature of government published indices; and to the paucity of well-trained accountants.

Without reference to this factor, it would not be possible to explain accounting differences in several countries severely affected by it. However, this factor is of only little assistance in explaining accounting differences in Europe. Nevertheless, the valuation of fixed assets particularly has been affected in some European countries, as discussed in section 2.5.

1.7 Theory

There has also been a strong influence in a few cases from theory, perhaps most obviously in the case of micro-economics in the Netherlands. Accounting theorists there (notably Theodore Limperg, Jr) had advanced the case that the users of financial statements would be given the fairest view of the performance and state of affairs of an individual company by allowing accountants to use judgment, in the context of that particular company, to select and present accounting figures. In particular, it was suggested that replacement cost information might give the best picture. The looseness of law and tax requirements, and the receptiveness of the profession to micro-economic ideas (no doubt partly because of their training by the academic theorists) has led to the present diversity of practice, the emphasis on 'fairness' through judgment, and the experimentation with and practice of replacement cost accounting.

In other countries, particularly in the English-speaking world, accounting practices seem to operate and develop without a clear theoretical framework.

1.8 Accidents

Many other influences have been at work in shaping accounting practices. Some are not indirect and subtle like the type of ownership of companies, but direct and external to accounting like the framing of a law in response to economic or political events. As an example outside Europe, the economic crisis in the USA in the late 1920s and early 1930s produced the Securities and Exchange Acts which have diverted US accounting from its previous course by introducing extensive disclosure requirements and control (usually by threat only) of accounting standards. As other examples, the introductions into Italy of Anglo-American accounting principles by choice of the government, and into Luxembourg of consolidation and detailed disclosure as a result of EC Directives are against all previous trends there. In Spain, the 'artificial' adoption of the accounting plan from France follows that latter country's adoption of it after influence by the occupying Germans in the early 1940s. Perhaps most obvious and least natural is the adoption of various British Companies Acts or of International Accounting Standards by developing countries with a negligible number of the sort of public companies or private shareholders which have given rise to the financial reporting practices contained in these laws or standards. In its turn, the UK in 1981 enacted uniform formats derived from the 1965 *Aktiengesetz* of West Germany because of EC requirements. For their part, Roman law countries are now having to grapple with the 'true and fair view' (see section 2.1).

1.9 Summary and Conclusion

This chapter has discussed some of the influences on the development of European financial reporting practices. The importance of the mix of users of accounting information seems clear; it has a large part to play in the emergence of the dominant source of rules for accounting practice. In many continental European countries, the importance of governments as collectors of taxation or controllers of the economy, has led to the dominance of company laws, commercial codes and tax regulations. In other countries, the effective control of financial reporting practice has been exercised by the accounting profession. This was first seen as a vague corpus of 'best' or 'accepted' practices, and later has been refined with the issue of detailed accounting standards. However, these standards are still loosely-drawn documents which permit considerable flexibility and the use of judgment. The interests of private shareholders as users of financial statements has been a continuing background pressure on the profession as it develops standard practice.

As a result of international harmonisation, much of it directly caused by the EC, many European countries are finding 'fairness' and audit thrust upon them; and the UK, Ireland and the Netherlands are receiving many detailed financial reporting rules into law. This development cuts across the fundamental causes of differences that we have been looking at. However, at least before this influence was widely felt, it is clear that the same countries are generally found together for most of the factors discussed above. This observation leads on to the thought of classification of countries (see Chapter 3). At this point we might note that an interesting exception to the otherwise clear pattern of countries is the Netherlands. Although, the Netherlands has a Roman legal system and few listed companies, if one studies its commercial, maritime history it bears considerable similarities to England's. Also, although the number of listed companies is small, some of those companies are very large and are the basis of an active stock exchange. At any rate, when it comes to taxation and the profession, the Netherlands appears to fit fairly well with the UK and Ireland (or the USA) as opposed to the continental European group.

References

Flint, D (1982) *A True and Fair View*, Gee, London.
Frank, W G (1979) 'An empirical analysis of international accounting principles', *Journal of Accounting Research*, Autumn.

Mueller, G G (1967) *International Accounting*, Macmillan, New York, part 1.

Nobes, C W (1986) 'New Laws for Old', *Accountancy*, December.

Nobes, C W and R H Parker (1985) *Comparative International Accounting*, Philip Allan.

Nobes, C W (1988) Interpreting US Financial Statements, Butterworths.

Stamp, E (1980) *Corporate Reporting: Its Future Evolution*, Canadian Institute of Chartered Accountants, Toronto.

Tweedie, D P and G Whittington (1984) *The Debate on Inflation Accounting*, Cambridge University Press.

CHAPTER 2

European Differences in Financial Reporting

To some extent, differences in financial reporting have already been discussed in Chapter 1 while examining the causes of the differences. This applies particularly to the first two headings below, which are therefore dealt with briefly here. Also, it should be noted that many factors overlap with others. For example, a discussion of conservatism tends to overlap with discussions of the accruals convention or of fairness, because the former tends to drive out the others.

This chapter discusses the broad headings under which European differences in financial reporting may be found. More detail of specific practices is given in Chapters 5 to 8. The intention here is not primarily to examine accounting practices country by country; that is done elsewhere (eg Nobes and Parker, 1985).

2.1 Fairness

The degree to which accountants and auditors search for 'fairness' as opposed to correctness or legality has differed substantially internationally. This was discussed in Chapter 1 and was linked to (i) a predominance of outside shareholders as providers of finance, and (ii) the lack of interference of law or taxation in financial reporting.

Until the 1980s, the laws of the UK, Ireland and the Netherlands were alone in the EC in requiring fairness or faithfulness from audited financial statements. On the one hand this elevates judgment of particular circumstances above uniform rules, but on the other it can be a far more onerous requirement for directors and auditors. It can, of course, also lead to the abuse of flexibility by directors because of the vagueness of 'fair'.

A related concept is 'substance over form', an expression usually associated with the USA. In an attempt to 'present fairly', accountants have come to the view that it is necessary to try to account for the economic substance of events rather than for the legal form. For example, it is deemed necessary to capitalise assets obtained on finance leases as though they had been bought.

A concern with fairness also lies behind the Dutch experimentation and use of replacement cost valuation, and the agonised attempts in the English-speaking world since the late 1960s to replace or supplement historical cost accounting.

The requirement of the EC's Fourth Directive that 'true and fair' should override detailed rules in all member states may lead to a mask of uniformity that conceals the unchanged old differences. For example, the requirement that French financial statements should give an *image fidèle* from 1984 involved changes in the law and in audit reports, but French accounting seemed little altered.

Similarly, in West Germany, until 1987 financial statements there was still requirement for fairness or for substance over form. Financial reporting was still an exercise in accurate bookkeeping which had to satisfy detailed rules and the scrutiny of the tax inspector. The recent requirement for French and German accounts to be 'fair' has largely been met by extra disclosures rather than a change in the presentation of numbers in the financial statements. This may make matters *worse* for Anglo-Saxon readers of financial statements, who may be misled by the increased superficial similarities.

2.2 Taxation

The influence of taxation has been discussed in Chapter 1 as a cause of differences in financial reporting. In most continental European countries, it is one of the enemies of fairness. In its effects on depreciation, bad debt provisions and some asset valuations it is a major example of differences in financial reporting.

2.3 Conservatism and Accruals

Another traditional adversary of fairness is conservatism. Perhaps because of the different mix of users in different countries, conservatism is of differing strength. For example, the importance of banks in West Germany may be a reason for greater conservatism in reporting. It is widely held that bankers are more interested in 'rock-bottom' figures in order to satisfy themselves that long-term loans are safe. At the same time, the consequent lack of those interested in a 'fair' view reduces the importance of the accruals convention which would normally modify conservatism.

In the UK it is now more usual to refer to the concept of 'prudence' (as in SSAP 2 and, now, company law). In many cases, accounting standards are the compromise treaties which settle a battle between conservatism and the accruals concept. For example, it is not fully conservative to allow the capitalisation of any development expenditure as in SSAP 13, but it may be reasonably prudent under certain conditions. A similar argument applies to the taking of profit on long-term contracts as in SSAP 9.

Continental European conservatism is of a more stringent variety, as may be illustrated by a study of published accounts. The annual report of *AEG-Telefunken* 1987 will be examined here. The evidence of conservatism in such reports depends upon the events of the year and the style of the companies' reports, thus it is not possible to organise a consistent survey. However, this report seems to be broadly representative of practice of large companies in Germany and is only presented as an example of the type of evidence available. The quotations below come from page 30 of the report and are designed to give an impression of the conservatism. Reports of other years would provide similar quotations.

Inventories: 'Raw materials . . . are valued at the lower cost and a lower value, to the extent that it is economically required or permissable.'
'Anticipated losses are fully provided for. . . . All anticipated risks from slow-moving and obsolete inventories are covered by appropriate write-downs.'

Debtors: 'Receivables and other assets have been valued after providing for all known risks. . . . In addition, the collection risk is covered by a general allowance for doubtful debts.'

Sundry Provisions: 'All anticipated risks are taken into account in the valuation of other accruals.'

Foreign Debt: 'Liabilities in foreign currencies [are held] at the higher rate of the exchange rate at the time of acquisition or at year end.'

Depreciation: (from an earlier year's report)   'Special provisions have been made where there are risks due to economic factors and obsolescence.'

As a postscript, it may be noted that many investment analysts greatly increase a Germany company's profit figures by a series of adjustments before comparing it to a UK figure (see occasional papers on Earnings per Share by *Deutsche Vereinigung für Finanzanalyse und Anlageberatung*). However, matters have 'improved' somewhat since the Aktiengesetz. Before that, it was suggested (Semler, 1962) that:

> 'If the non-existence of a contingency cannot be absolutely determined, then in the interest of protecting the creditor, it must be assumed that such a contingency exists.'

This greater conservatism in continental Europe seems to be a long-run phenomenon. Davidson and Kohlmeier (1966) and Abel (1969) noted that profit figures would be consistently lower in France, Sweden, Germany and the Netherlands (when use of replacement cost was assumed) if similar companies' accounts were merely adjusted for differences in inventory and depreciation practices from those used in the USA or the UK. Gray (1980) examined France, West Germany and the UK in order to produce an index of conservatism. He concluded that French and German companies are significantly more conservative or pessimistic than UK companies (p 69).

A further example of the protection of creditors is the use of statutory or legal reserves in most continental countries. These are undistributable reserves that are set up out of declared profits. They are an extra protection for creditors above the normal Anglo-American maintenance of capital rules. In France, West Germany and Italy a company is required to appropriate 5% tranches (10% in Italy) of its annual profit until the statutory reserve reaches 10% of issued share capital (20% in Italy).

A particular piece of evidence of the lack of importance of the accruals concept (though not of conservatism) in Germany is the absence of a 'provision for proposed dividends' in annual balance sheets. Since there needs to be an AGM to bring the dividends into legal existence, they cannot exist at the balance sheet date! French balance sheets compromise between the German and British views by presenting the liabilities-and-capital side of a balance sheet in two columns: before and after allocation of net profits.

There are some more remarks concerning conservatism and accruals in section 2.4 below.

2.4 Provisions and Reserves

The distinction between provisions and reserves is important for financial reporting because the former are charges against profit, whereas the latter are appropriations of profit. The influences which lead to a proliferation of significant provisions appear to be conservatism and rigid but generous tax regulations. Both these factors have been discussed, and their effects on provisions mentioned. The result of such provision-accounting may be that the accruals convention and 'fairness' are partially overridden; this in turn may result in income smoothing.

The use of accelerated depreciation in the financial accounts is an example of over-provision. The lack of provision for bad debts merely because it is not allowed for tax purposes is an example of under-provision. Provisions for risks and contingencies which fluctuate in reverse relationship with profits are examples of income smoothing. This will be illustrated using several different years of the annual reports of French and German companies.

In the 1983 Annual Report of CFP, there is a Chartered Accountants' Report (p A5) which notes that in the UK 'the provision for contingencies would be classified as a reserve'. In earlier years, there were even more revealing remarks in the versions of the annual reports of CFP that were specially prepared for UK readers:

> 'Depreciation of property, plant and equipment was F 2274 million vs F 2283 million in 1976. Provision amounts were lower in 1977 than in 1976, especially because cash flow reflected on the French market did not allow constitution of a provision for foreign exchange fluctuations at the same level as in 1976.' (1977, p 22)

> 'Taking into account these items, income for the year was F 111 million, to which must be added a deduction of F 90 million from the provision for contingencies. Income finally amounts to F 201 million ... but includes lower exceptional income.' (1977, p 23)

> 'Following the usual effect of amounts set aside to or written back from depreciation and provisions and an allocation of F 800 million to reconstitute the provision for contingencies, net income for the year totalled F 971 million.' (1979, p 23)

As a result of the 1983 Law requiring fairness, CFP transferred its contingency 'provision' to 'reserves' in 1984. However, not all large French companies have followed this practice.

Turning to Germany, remarks concerning provisions have already been made in the section on conservatism. Using AEG again as an example, the 1987 profit and loss account (see Table 2.1 opposite) shows a 'net income' of exactly zero for 1986 and 1987. The inevitable conclusion must be that the

Table 2.1   Consolidated Statement of Income of AEG Group for 1987

	1987		1986	
	Million DM	**Million DM**	**Million DM**	**Million DM**
Sales	**11,660**		**11,220**	
Change in inventories and work capitalised	+ 276		+ 137	
Total Operating Performance		**11,936**		**11,357**
Other operating income	+ 533		+ 464	
Cost of materials	− 5,376		− 5,212	
Personnel expenses	− 4,642		− 4,489	
Depreciation of intangible and fixed assets	− 357		− 295	
Other operating expenses	− 2,050		− 1,760	
Investment results (net)	+ 16		+ 2	
Interest income (net)	+ 26		+ 1	
Result from other financial investments and current assets securities (net)	− 3			
		− 11,853		− 11,289
Results from Ordinary Business Activity		**+ 83**		**+ 68**
Extraordinary results	− 19		−	
Taxes on income	− 16		− 25	
Other taxes	− 48		− 43	
		− 83		− 68
Net Income		**−**		**−**
Withdrawals from transfers to revenue reserves	+ 5		− 12	
Minority interest in income and losses	− 5		+ 12	
Group Result		**−**		**−**

income statement is calculated by working backwards from the 'net income' of zero. This is income smoothing on an heroic scale.

It appears that, in Italy and Spain, the Commercial Codes (which would certainly allow greater use of the accruals convention) have been overridden to a large extent by the need to satisfy the requirements of tax inspectors. Only recently, and particularly in Italy, have tax reforms and stronger accounting principles allowed the use of 'fairer' provisions of various types.

In the UK, provisions for depreciation and for non-specific bad debts are not affected by tax requirements. Provisions for risks and contingencies are rare and usually associated with cases where a liability is specifically identified and probable. Broadly speaking, these practices prevail in the rest of the English-speaking world and in the Netherlands. However, there is an important exception in the treatment of deferred tax, which is fully provided for in the USA, Canada, Australia, and the Netherlands, but (since the late 1970s) not in the UK and Ireland (see Chapter 7).

2.5 Valuation Bases

There is great international variation in the predominant basis of valuation and the degree to which there is experimentation and supplementation with alternative measures. In a country with detailed legal rules and a coincidence of tax and commercial accounting it must be expected that the predominant valuation system will be one that involves as little judgment as possible. Flexibility and judgment would make it difficult for auditors to determine whether the law had been obeyed and they might lead to arbitrary taxation demands. Thus, in a country such as West Germany, it seems unsurprising that the required method of valuation is a strict form of historical cost.

At the other extreme is the Netherlands. Some Dutch companies (eg Philips) have published replacement cost financial statements since the early 1950s. Although this remains minority practice, many Dutch companies partially or supplementarily use replacement costs or other current values. Dutch practice reflects the influence of microeconomic theory and a striving after fairness.

In between these two extremes, UK 'rules' allow a chaotic state of affairs where some companies revalue, some of the time, using a variety of methods. Also, there has been experimentation with current cost accounting, normally as supplementary statements. This is the story for most of the English-speaking world, except that the USA and Canada keep to historical cost in the main financial statements; this is because of the influence of the SEC.

In France, Spain and Italy, where there is much tax and other government influence, there has also been more inflation than in Germany and a greater drive towards the creation of large and efficient equity capital markets. Governments and stock exchange bodies in these countries have appreciated the effects of inflation on historical cost accounting and have required revaluations. However, this creates severe problems in such countries (see Chapter 6).

This fundamental difference in methods of asset valuation means that international comparisons become difficult for net assets, shareholders' funds and many ratios.

2.6 Consolidation

The prevalence of consolidation has varied dramatically among EC countries. Most practices seem to have first enjoyed widespread adoption in the USA: for example, the normal acquisition (purchase) method of accounting for a business combination. There are examples of consolidation at least as far back as the 1890s, and it was widespread practice by the early 1920s. The various factors that might have caused this early development in the USA may help to explain the diversity in the EC. The US factors may have been:

(*i*)   a wave of mergers at the turn of the century, leading to the carrying on of business by groups of companies;
(*ii*)   the prevalence of the holding company (which merely owns investments) as opposed to the parent company (which is one of the operating companies of the group);
(*iii*) the lack of a legal requirement for holding/parent company balance sheets, unlike the UK or German law for example;
(*iv*)   the lack of legal or other barriers to the emergence of new techniques, and the existence of innovative professionals;
(*v*)   use of consolidation for tax purposes (1917 to 1934);
(*vi*)   acceptance of consolidation by the New York Stock Exchange (1919).

In the UK consolidation came later. Holding companies were perhaps less important until during the First World War, although there was a UK wave of mergers at the turn of the century. Nevertheless, UK mergers did not usually involve holding companies. Also, tax never moved to a consolidated basis in the UK. It used to be commonly held that Nobel Industries (ICI) pioneered consolidation in the early 1920s and Dunlop in the 1930s. However, Edwards and Webb (1984) have found much earlier evidence. The Stock Exchange required consolidation as a condition of new issues from 1939; and consolidation became almost universal after the Companies Act 1948.

In the Netherlands, consolidation was also practised by the 1930s. However, in most of continental Europe, consolidation is either a recent development or still very rare. In Germany, consolidation was made obligatory by the 1965 *Aktiengesetz* for public companies. However, foreign subsidiaries did not need to be (and generally were not) consolidated, and the use of the equity method for associated companies was not allowed. Further, there were important differences from Anglo-American practice in the use of an economic (rather than a legal) basis for 'the group', and a yearly calculation of 'differences arising on consolidation' based on book values rather than a once-for-all calculation of goodwill based on fair values. West Germany implemented the Seventh Directive in 1985, thus removing most of these differences from 1990 (see Chapter 8).

In France, before 1985, there was no law on consolidation, and consolidation had been very rare. However, the formation of COB in the late 1960s and the influence of Anglo-American practices, due to the presence of international firms and the desire of some French companies for listings on the Exchanges of London or New York, caused a gradual increase in consolidation by listed companies (see Table 2.2 overleaf). Naturally, in a country where there is no tradition of professional accounting measurement standards, in cases where there were no law or tax requirements, practice has

Table 2.2   Number of Listed French Companies Publishing Consolidated Financial Statements

	At least a consolidated balance sheet	Consolidated balance sheet plus consolidated profit and loss account
1967	22	15
1968	44	25
1969	64	39
1970	74	42
1971	104	76
1972	163	121
1973	216	161
1974	232	183
1975	267	213
1976	292	246
1977	319	267
1978	328	289
1979	351	305

Source: Commission des Opérations de Bourse, Annual Reports.

been very varied. The *Conseil National de la Comptabilité*, a government body with responsibility for the *Plan*, issued guidelines in 1968 and 1978. However, these guidelines were not followed exactly. In 1985 a law was passed to require listed companies to publish consolidated financial statements. Other companies must follow by 1990.

In Belgium and Spain, until the 1980s, consolidation was very rare. In Italy, CONSOB has been encouraging consolidation, but it has been rare even for listed companies. The result of lack of consolidation in these many EC countries is that outside investors or lenders (particularly foreigners) have grossly inadequate information, even about large listed groups. The situation in Switzerland is broadly the same. Tables 2.3 and 2.4 opposite show the best available set of accounts for a large Swiss group. It appears that there are no buildings or machines, no sales or wages. This is because the best available accounts are those of the holding company, whereas all the operations are performed in subsidiaries. Of course, it is even more confusing when *part* of the group's operations are performed by the parent.

Why have most continental European countries been so far behind the UK and the USA in the development of consolidation? The reasons may include:

(*i*)   the existence of many legal requirements that made the preparation of individual company balance sheets compulsory and militated against new ideas;

(*ii*)   the lack of a large or strong profession to innovate;

(*iii*)   the lesser importance of big business and holding companies;

(*iv*)   the importance of bankers and creditors who might oppose consolidation on the grounds that it confuses legal liabilities;

(*v*)   the importance (as users of accounts) of the revenue authorities, and in some cases governments, who prefer to do their own manipulations of the accounts of individual companies;

Table 2.3   Balance Sheet of Holzstoff Holding Inc at 31.12.1986

		SFr
Assets	Investments	73 523 170.—
	Loans to group companies	33 068 800.—
	Accounts receivable	2 839 436.34
	Securities	3 328 330.—
	Cash and cash items	46 399 694.46
	Total	159 159 430.80
Liabilities and equity	Share capital	40 000 000.—
	Legal reserves	4 840 000.—
	Special reserves	22 200 000.—
	Debentures* 4 1/2, due 1992	15 000 000.—
	4 3/4, due 1993	20 000 000.—
	Accounts payable	138 476.80
	Provisions	48 209 590.—
	Retained earnings	282 860.36
	Earnings	8 488 503.64
	Total	159 159 430.80

Table 2.4   Income Statement of Holzstoff Holding Inc for 1986

		SFr
Revenues	Revenue from investments	12 437 023.13
	Interest income	2 967 437.96
	Other revenue	388 249.95
	Dissolution of the provision for cost of group reorganisation	—
	Total	15 792 711.04
Expenditures	Interest expense	1 625 000.—
	Taxes	1 646 207.40
	Depreciation and provisions	4 033 000.—
	Cost of group reorganisation	—
	Earnings	8 488 503.64
	Total	15 792 711.04

(*vi*) the relative lack of importance of shareholders who may want an overall 'economic' view.

One of the effects of this rarity of consolidation was that the EC's major draft law on financial reporting (the Fourth Directive) was adopted in 1978

23

without any recognition of group accounting. Presumably, when the first draft was published in 1971, a requirement to consolidate would have been hopelessly controversial.

However, as we have seen, the stock exchange bodies and governments of most EC countries have begun to take actions to require listed or public companies to consolidate. This is designed to make their domestic capital markets more efficient and to internationalise the flows of capital. It is of course logical to direct the consolidation rules at those companies where outside providers of finance are important. The Seventh Directive of the EC (adopted in 1983) requires consolidation rules by 1990 (see Chapter 8).

2.7 Uniformity and Accounting Plans

The degree to which financial reporting is uniform among companies within a country varies. Before the early 1980s when the EC's harmonising measures began to take effect, the variations were greater. Uniformity can exist in three main areas: formats of financial statements, accounting principles and disclosure requirements. Clearly, where there are detailed legal rules in any or all of these areas, there will be a high degree of uniformity.

In order to examine the emergence of uniformity, one should probably start with Germany. It was for internal, cost accounting purposes that uniform formats were first developed. They could also be used for inter-firm comparisons within an industry. It appears that the first comprehensive chart of accounts was published in Germany in 1911 and that such charts were used by industry in the First World War. Under the National Socialists, the ascendant ideology of controlling the economy led naturally to the compulsory adoption of charts of accounts.

In France, the needs of the Economics Ministry in its role as controller of the French economy were seen to be well served by the use of uniform accounting encouraged by the occupying German forces in the early 1940s. Consequently, such a system has been in use in France throughout the post-war years. The first full version of the *plan comptable général* was produced in 1947, and revised versions were issued in 1957 and (as partial implementation of the Fourth Directive) in 1982. The *plan* exists in many versions for different industries. It comprises a chart of accounts, definitions of terms, model financial statements and rules for measurement and valuation. The chart of accounts controls a company's internal bookkeeping system. It is a decimalised system of nominal ledger codes. The first two digits of the current French chart are shown in Table 2.5 on p 26. However, the detail goes down to five digits. This system makes work easier for auditors, tax inspectors and accountants as they move from one company to another. It also speeds the training of bookkeepers; and it is an obvious micro-computer application.

The influence of the *plan comptable* is all-pervasive. The chart must be completed each year for national statistical purposes; the tax returns are based on the plan; published financial statements use the model formats (see Chapter 5); and all the former use the standard definitions and measurement rules. The *plan* even stretches to cost and management accounting.

Its use for central statistical purposes is very obvious. A government economist in Paris can collect charts for all companies and add together all amounts under a particular decimalised code in order to find the total investment in a particular type of fixed asset, defined in a standardised way.

Naturally, as the government is historically the main user of accounting information in its capacities as economic controller, tax collector and provider of state capital, the *plan* is controlled by a government body: the *Conseil National de la Comptabilité*. It is enforced through a company law of 1983.

In Belgium, part of the process of preparing for the implementation of the Fourth Directive during the 1970s was the introduction of an accounting plan in 1976, not dissimilar to the French one. The Belgians had used a chart of accounts for some industries during the inter-war years, and had experienced full use of it during the early 1940s. The *plan comptable minimum normalisé* is now compulsory. However, unlike the French *plan*, the Belgian one mainly concerns charts of accounts, which are to be sent to the Banque Nationale.

In Spain, an accounting plan has been progressively introduced. The Ministry of Public Finance established the Institute of Accounting Planning in 1973 which has produced several versions of the plan for different sectors. As in France, the plan consists of a chart of accounts, a set of definitions, formats for annual accounts and valuation principles. The headings of the decimalised chart of accounts are in the same order as the French chart, though the subheadings vary to some extent. The plan began by being voluntary. Then, by an Act of December 1973, the plan had to be used for those companies who wished to revalue. This continued for the 1978 and 1979 fiscal revaluations (somewhat like the French revaluations of similar date). However, by an Order of 14 January 1980, companies covered by plans already in issue must now comply with the plans.

Greece has also adopted an accounting plan. In this case, and in France and Spain, the *plans* include uniform financial statements for publication. In Belgium and Germany, uniform financial statements are required instead by company law. An interesting irony is that West Germany is now the only country of the five not to have a compulsory accounting plan.

In Anglo-Saxon countries, there has generally been much less uniformity. As far as formats for financial statements are concerned, there were no rules in law (before the 1981 UK Act and the 1983 Netherlands Act) and virtually none in accounting standards. The requirements of the Fourth Directive were based on German law and were revolutionary compared to previous Anglo-Dutch rules. But even now, there remains much more flexibility in the UK, Ireland and the Netherlands than in the rest of the EC.

Turning to accounting principles, the control by company law, tax law or accounting plan has been substantial in most EC countries. Though, again, in the UK, Ireland and the Netherlands, there have traditionally been no rules in company law apart from 'fairness'. Instead, the accountancy profession has been influential in inventing and policing the rules of valuation and measurement. In the UK and Ireland, the Accounting Standards Committee is controlled by the professional bodies. In the Netherlands, guidelines are published by the Council for Annual Reporting (*Raad voor Jaarrekening*) in which the Netherlands Institute of Registered Accountants plays the most influential role.

Standards and guidelines in these latter countries are not legally binding. In the UK and Ireland, non-compliance should lead to an audit qualification; in the Netherlands not even that. However, the legal requirement for 'fairness' would be likely to be interpreted by a court with the aid of standards. In the Netherlands there is a special Enterprise Chamber of the

Table 2.5 Extract from French Chart of Accounts

Class 1	Class 2	Class 3	Class 4	Class 5	Class 6	Class 7	Class 8	Class 9
Capital accounts (capital, loans and similar creditors)	Fixed asset accounts	Stock and work-in progress accounts	Personal accounts	Financial accounts	Expense accounts	Income accounts	Special accounts	Cost accounts
10 Capital and reserves	20 Intangible assets	30	40 Suppliers and related accounts	50 Trade investments	60 Purchases and stock movements (supplies and goods for resale)	70 Sales of goods and	80 Contingent assets and liabilities	90 Reciprocal accounts
11 Profit or loss brought forward	21 Tangible assets	31 Raw materials	41 Trade debtors and related accounts	51 Banks financial and similar institutions	61 Purchases from sub-contractors and external charges (related to investment)	71 Movements in finished goods during the accounting period	81[a]	91 Cost reclassifications
12 Profit or loss for the financial year	22 Fixed assets under concession	32 Other consumables	42 Employees and related accounts	52	62 Other external charges (related to operations)	72 Work performed by the undertaking for its own purposes and capitalised	82[a]	92 Cost analysis centres
13 Investment grants	23 Fixed assets in course of construction	33 Work in progress (goods)	43 Social security and other public agencies	52 Cash in hand	63 Taxes, direct and indirect	73 Net income recognised on long-term contracts	83[a]	93 Manufacturing costs

14 Provisions created for tax purposes	24	34 Work-in progress (services)	44 The Government and other public bodies	54 Imprest accounts and credits	64 Staff costs	74 Operating subsidies	84(a)	94 Stocks
15 Provisions for liabilities and charges	25	35 Finished goods	45 Accounts current—group companies and proprietors	55	65 Other operating charges	75 Other operating income	85(a)	95 Costs of goods sold
16 Loans and similar creditors	26 Participating interests and debts relating thereto	36	46 Sundry debtors and creditors	56	66 Financial costs	76 Financial income	86 Intra-company exchanges of goods and services (charges)	96 Standard cost variances
17 Debts related to participating interests	27 Other financial assets	37 Goods for resale	47 Suspense accounts	57 Internal transfers	67 Extra-ordinary	77 Extra-ordinary	87 Intra-company exchanges of goods and services (income)	97 Difference in accounting treatments
18 Branch and inter company accounts	28 Provisions for depreciation of fixed assets	38	48 Prepayments and accruals	58	68 Depreciation amortisation, transfers to	78 Depreciation and provisions written back	88	98 Manufacturing profit and loss account
19	29 Provisions for loss in value of fixed assets	39 Provisions for loss in value of stocks and work-in progress	49 Provisions for loss in value on personal accounts	59 Provisions for loss in value on financial accounts	69 Profit sharing by employees, taxes on profits and similar items	79 Charges transferred	89	99 Internal transfers

Court of Justice especially for accounting cases. Nevertheless, there has been plenty of room for variety in those Anglo-Saxon countries in the EC and elsewhere. However, the implementation of the Fourth Directive has introduced many detailed rules into law for the first time. This has somewhat increased uniformity, but mainly it has raised problems between law and standards.

The remaining potential area of uniformity is disclosure requirements. One difference between Franco-German and Anglo-Saxon practice is that companies in the former countries tend to restrict their disclosures to legal requirements, except when seeking to raise Anglo-American finance. In the UK and Ireland, the basic disclosures required by law are substantial and lead to considerable uniformity. However, other disclosures required by or recommended by the profession, or experimented with by individual companies, are common. This leads to a certain degree of variation.

2.8 Shareholder Orientation of Financial Statements

The first section of this chapter discussed the connection between 'fairness' and the predominance of outside shareholders. Shareholder orientation spreads further than accounting principles; it affects the formats of financial statements. At its most obvious, the general use of a vertical format in the UK and Ireland rather than a horizontal format in West Germany or France suggests a greater shareholder-orientation in the former countries. This is because the vertical format allows the presentation of working capital and net worth, and it contrasts net worth with shareholders' funds.

However, even in the horizontal version of the balance sheet (see Chapter 5), the UK version has greater shareholder-orientation than a traditional German format: for example, it shows all the elements of shareholders' funds together, rather than showing the year's net profit as a separate item at the bottom of the balance sheet (or a loss at the bottom of the assets side!) as did the 1965 *Aktiengesetz*. The greater German interest in the double-entry aspects of the balance sheet was also demonstrated by the presentation of 'provisions for bad debts' as a liability (rather than being deducted from debtors), and 'called up share capital not paid' as the first asset (rather than as a debtor). The formats introduced in Germany by the 1985 legislation to implement the Fourth Directive removed many of these differences, but other continental countries still retain them.

The usual German style profit and loss account (see Chapter 5) is also probably less useful for decision-making than the normal Anglo-Saxon concentration on gross profit, net profit and 'earnings'. This is in addition to the problem of income smoothing discussed earlier. Further, disclosed calculations of earnings per share are normal only in the Anglo-Saxon world.

2.9 Conclusion

The eight areas of difference discussed above are amongst the more important variations in financial reporting practice, though they do not amount to a complete list. What is clear is that a reader would be seriously misled if he compared financial statements from apparently similar companies from various countries. The first step is to be aware that the differences exist. Later chapters suggest adjustments that might be made.

References

Abel, R (1969) 'A comparative simulation of German and US accounting principles', *Journal of Accounting Research*, Spring.

Davidson, S and Kohlmeier, J (1966) 'A measure of the impact of some foreign accounting principles', *Journal of Accounting Research*, Autumn.

Edwards, J R and Webb, K M (1984) 'The development of group accounting in the UK to 1933', *Accounting Historians Journal*, Spring.

Gray, S J (1980) 'The impact of international accounting differences from a security-analysis perspective: some European evidence', *Journal of Accounting Research*, Spring.

Nobes, C W and Parker, R H (1985) *Comparative International Accounting*, Philip Allan.

Semler, J (1962) 'The German accountant's approach to safeguarding investors' and creditors' interests', paper at the Eighth International Congress of Accountants, reprinted in *The Australian Accountant*, September.

CHAPTER 3

Classification of Financial Reporting in Europe

Chapters 1 and 2 have discussed the causes and main examples of differences in financial reporting practices in Europe. From this it is clear that, although no two countries have identical rules and practices, some countries seem to form pairs or larger groupings with reasonably similar financial reporting. If this is so, it may be possible to establish a classification. Such an activity is a basic step in many disciplines other than accounting. Before attempting a European accounting classification, it may be useful to make short surveys of classification in other disciplines, of the normal rules for classifications, of the purposes of classifications, and of previous attempts in accounting.

3.1 Purpose, Rules and Examples

Classification is one of the basic tools of a scientist. The Mendeleev table of elements and the Linnaean system of classification are fundamental to chemistry and biology. Classification should sharpen description and analysis. It should reveal underlying structures and enable prediction of the properties of an element based on its place in a classification.

Different types of classification are possible, from the simplest form of dichotomous grouping (eg things black versus things white) or rank ordering (eg by height of students in a class) to more complex dimensioning (such as the periodic table) or systematising (such as the Linnaean system).

It may now be useful to examine traditional methods of classification in areas close to accounting. There have been classifications of political, economic and legal systems. For example, political systems have been grouped into political democracies, tutelary democracies, modernising oligarchies, totalitarian oligarchies and traditional oligarchies. Economic systems have been divided into capitalism, socialism, communism and fascism. A more recent classification is: traditional economies, market economies and planned economies.

One set of authors, while classifying legal systems, has supplied practical criteria for determining whether two systems are in the same group. Systems are said to be in the same group if 'someone educated in . . . one law will then be capable, without much difficulty, of handling (the other)' (David and Brierley, 1978, p 20). Also, the two systems must not be 'founded on opposed philosophical, political or economic principles'. The second criterion ensures that systems in the same group not only have superficial characteristics, but also have similar fundamental structures and are likely to react to new circumstances in similar ways. Using these criteria a four-group legal

30

classification was obtained: Romano-Germanic, Common Law, Socialist and Philosophical-Religious.

In all the above examples, the type of classification used was rudimentary, involving no more than splitting systems into a few groups. The groups within the classifications were sometimes not precisely defined nor exhaustive. Also, the method used to determine and fill the groups was little more than subjective classification based on personal knowledge or descriptive literature. These shortcomings are very difficult to avoid because of the complexity and 'greyness' in the social sciences.

3.2 Classification in Accounting

The reasons for wanting to classify financial reporting 'systems' into groups include the general reasons for classification in any science, as outlined above. In this case, classification should be an efficient way of describing and comparing different systems. It should help to chart the progress of one system as it moves from one group to another, and the progress of ideas of a dominant country's system, by noting the other national systems grouped around it. The activity involved in preparing a classification should encourage precision. Moreover, in the social sciences, classification may be used to help shape development rather than merely to describe how and why things are. For example, classification should facilitate a study of the logic of and the difficulties facing European harmonisation. Classification should also assist in the training of accountants and auditors who operate internationally. Further, a developing country might be better able to understand the available types of financial reporting, and which one would be most appropriate for it, by seeing which other countries use particular systems. Also, it should be possible for a country to predict the problems that it is about to face and the solutions that might work by looking at other countries in its group.

Early Classification and Recent Descriptions

Early attempts at classification and more recent descriptions of different national systems form the background to modern classifications. Of the former, there is evidence for a three-group classification (UK, US and continental) being used from the beginning of the twentieth century (Hatfield, reprinted 1966). More recent descriptions and analyses like those by Zeff (1972), Price Waterhouse (1973, 1975 and 1979) and the AICPA (1964 and 1975) provide the raw material for classification.

Mueller's Classification

Mueller (1967) broke new ground by preparing a suggested classification of accounting systems into four patterns of development. This was a simple grouping which is not accompanied by an explanation of the method used to obtain it. However, the 'range of four is considered sufficient to embrace accounting as it is presently known and practised in various parts of the globe' (Mueller 1967, p 2). Each group was illustrated by one or two examples. It may well be that it is not reasonable to expect a more sophisticated classification, particularly in a pioneering work, and that Mueller's informed judgment was one of the best methods of classification available.

Mueller stresses that the types of accounting rules which exist in a country are a product of economic, political and other environments, which have determined the nature of the system. This also suggests that other countries' rules would not be appropriate to that country and that rules must be chosen to fit a country's needs. Consequently, doubt is cast on the possibility and usefulness of harmonisation.

Mueller's four groups, which are usefully summarised in a later work (Choi and Mueller 1984) are:

1   Accounting within a Macroeconomic Framework.   In this case, accounting has developed as an adjunct of national economic policies. We might expect such financial accounting to stress value-added statements, to encourage income smoothing, to be equivalent to tax accounting and to include social responsibility accounting. Sweden is said to be an example.

2   The Microeconomic Approach.   This approach can prosper in a market-oriented economy which has individual private businesses at the core of its economic affairs. The influence of microeconomics has led accounting to try to reflect economic reality in its measurement and valuations. This means that accounting rules must be sophisticated but flexible. Developments like replacement cost accounting will be accepted most readily in such systems. The Netherlands is suggested as an example.

3   Accounting as an Independent Discipline.   Systems of this sort have developed independently of governments or economic theories. Accounting has developed in business, has faced problems when they arrived, and has adopted solutions which worked. Theory is held in little regard and turned to only in emergencies or used *ex post* in an attempt to justify practical conclusions. Expressions such as 'generally accepted accounting principles' are typical. Mueller recognised the accounting systems of the UK and the USA as examples.

4   Uniform Accounting.   Such systems have developed where government have used accounting as a part of the administrative control of business. Accounting can be used to measure performance, allocate funds, assess the size of industries and resources, control prices, collect taxation, manipulate sectors of business, and so on. It involves standardisation of definitions, measurements and presentation. France is cited as an example.

Mueller was not classifying financial reporting systems directly, on the basis of differences in *practices*, but indirectly, on the basis of differences in the importance of economic, governmental and business factors in the development of particular systems. However, one might expect that systems which have developed in a similar way would have similar accounting practices.

Nevertheless, there are a few problems with Mueller's classification. The fact that there are only four exclusive groups and no hierarchy reduces the usefulness of the classification. In effect, the Netherlands is the only country in one of the groups and the classification does not show whether Dutch accounting is closer to UK accounting than it is to Swedish accounting. Similarly, the classification cannot include such facts as that West German accounting exhibits features which remind one of macroeconomic accounting as well as of uniform accounting.

Spheres of Influence

There have been some 'subjective' classifications based on 'spheres of influence'. Seidler (1967) suggested three groups: British, American and continental European. Also, the AAA's committee produced a subjective classification of 'zones of influence' on accounting systems (AAA 1977, pp 105 and 129–130). These are:

1 British
2 Franco-Spanish-Portuguese
3 German-Dutch
4 US
5 Communist

This classification is perhaps most useful in a discussion of developing countries. It seems less appropriate as a general method of classifying financial reporting. This is because it has no hierarchy and thus does not take account, for example, of the links between British and US accounting. Further, to call a group 'German–Dutch' seems very inappropriate as a way of classifying developed financial reporting systems, when examined in the light of the material in Chapters 1 and 2.

Classifications using Clustering

Other researchers have used the 1973 and the 1975 Price Waterhouse Surveys. For example, Nair and Frank (1980) divide the 1973 Survey's financial reporting characteristics into those relating to measurement and those relating to disclosure. This is a very useful differentiation, particularly because of the effect it has on the classification of countries like Germany which have advanced disclosure requirements. Using disclosure and measurement characteristics, Germany is classified in a 'US group'. However, by using 'measurement' characteristics only, Nair and Frank (1980) classify Germany in the continental European group. Table 3.1 below represents the classification using measurement characteristics. As yet there is no hierarchy, but the overall results do seem very plausible and fit well with the analysis in previous chapters of this book.

Table 3.1   Classification Based on Measurement Practices

British Commonwealth Model	Latin American Model	Continental European Model	United States Model
Australia	Argentina	Belgium	Canada
Bahamas	Bolivia	France	Japan
Eire	Brazil	Germany	Mexico
Fiji	Chile	Italy	Panama
Jamaica	Columbia	Spain	Philippines
Kenya	Ethiopia	Sweden	United States
Netherlands	India	Switzerland	
New Zealand	Paraguay	Venezuela	
Pakistan	Peru		
Rhodesia	South Africa		
Singapore	Uruguay		
Trinidad & Tobago			
United Kingdom			

Source: Nair and Frank (1980).

The suggestion is that, in a world-wide context, much of continental Europe can be seen as using the same system. However, the UK, Ireland and the Netherlands are noticeably different.

3.3   A New Approach

It would be possible to criticise the classifications discussed above for: (i) lack of precision in the definition of what is to be classified; (ii) lack of a model with which to compare the statistical results; (iii) lack of hierarchy which would add more subtlety to the portrayal of the size of differences between countries; and (iv) lack of judgment in the choice of 'important' discriminating features. Can these problems be remedied? The author attempted to solve them in his own researches relating to 14 developed countries (see Table 3.2 opposite and Nobes, 1983). This approach is adapted here for the 12 countries of the EC. (As may be seen from Table 3.2, the original study included the following EC countries: UK, Ireland, Netherlands, Belgium, France, West Germany, Italy and Spain.)

Definition

The scope of the work is defined as the classification of some European countries by the financial reporting practices of their *public companies*. The reporting practices are those concerned with *measurement and valuation*. It is public companies whose financial statements are generally available and whose practices can be most easily discovered. It is the international differences in reporting between such companies which are of main interest to shareholders, creditors, auditing firms, taxation authorities, managements and harmonising agencies. Measurement and valuation practices were chosen because these determine the size of the figures for profit, capital, total assets, liquidity and so on.

A Model with a Hierarchy

The hypothetical classification shown as Table 3.3 on p 36 is adapted from that proposed for a somewhat different group of countries in the previous study. The classification is based on the major background factors of law, tax and predominant users.

Classifications by others (eg Table 3.1) have contained separate groups but no hierarchy which would indicate the comparative distances between the groups. It may well be reasonable to classify the UK and the Netherlands in different groups, but it might be useful to demonstrate that these two groups are closely linked, compared to, say, continental European countries. The classification in Table 3.3 contains a hierarchy which borrows its labels from biology.

Table 3.3 suggests that there are two main types of financial reporting 'system' in Europe: the micro/professional and the macro/uniform. The former involves accountants in individual companies striving to present fair information to outside users, without detailed constraints of law or tax rules but with professional guidelines. The latter type has accounting mainly as a servant of the state, particularly for taxation purposes.

Table 3.2   A Hypothetical Classification of Financial Reporting Measurement Practices in Developed Western Countries

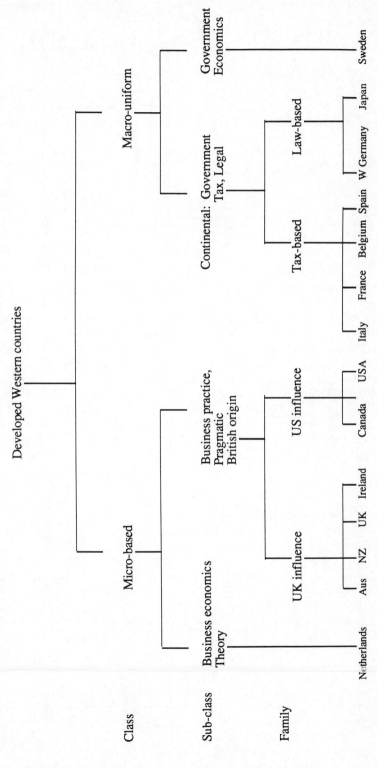

Table 3.3 Classification of Some European Countries

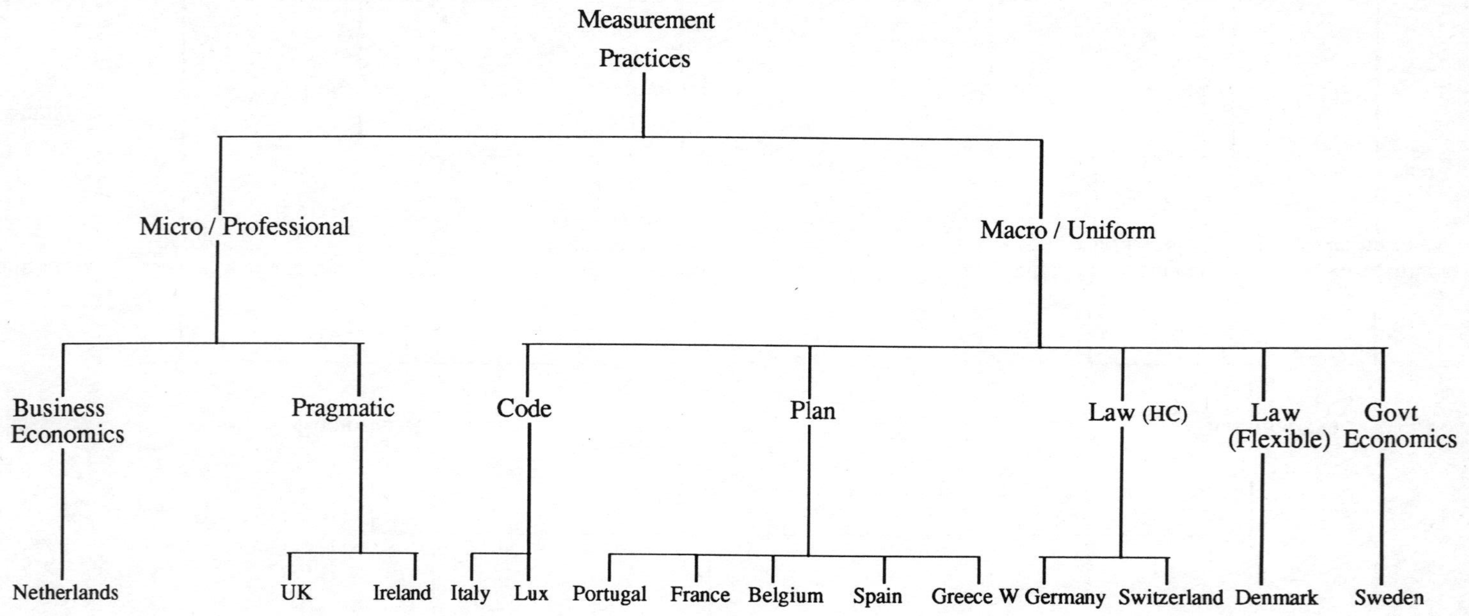

   The micro/professional side contains the Netherlands, the UK and Ireland (and, outside Europe, it also contains the USA, Australia, New Zealand and Canada). The Netherlands is even more free of rules than are the UK and Ireland, although the influence of micro-economic theory has led to use of replacement cost information to varying degrees.

   The macro/uniform side contains all other European countries. However, they can be divided into groups. For example, accounting plans are now the predominant source of detailed rules in France, Belgium, Spain and Greece. In West Germany and Denmark, company law is the major authority, but the former country has much stricter observance of historical cost values and tax-based depreciation. In Italy, Luxembourg and Portugal, tax rules are also a vital determinant of detailed practices. Other rules come from commercial codes rather than from accounting plans or company laws. In Sweden, the predominant influence seems to be the government as economic planner and tax collector.

   The purpose of Table 3.3 is to organise countries into groups by similarities of financial reporting measurement practices. This means that a knowledge of one country enables inferences to be drawn about others. The 'distance' between two countries is suggested by how far back up the classification it is necessary to go to reach a common point. This should be useful for those accountants and auditors who have to deal with financial reports from several European countries or who have to work in more than one country.

   Such a classification also prompts questions about whether harmonisation is desirable and possible. It is to this subject that we now turn.

References

AAA (1977) *Accounting Review, Supplement to Vol 52*, American Accounting Association.

AICPA (1964) *Professional Accounting in 25 Countires*, AICPA, New York.

AICPA (1975) *Professional Accounting in 30 Countries*, AICPA, New York.

Choi, F D S and Mueller, G G (1984) *International Accounting*, Prentice-Hall, ch 2.

David, R and Brierley, J E C (1978) *Major Legal Systems in the World Today*, Stevens, London.

Hatfield, H R (1966) 'Some variations in accounting practices in England, France, Germany and the US', *Journal of Accounting Research*, Autumn.

Mueller, G G (1967) *International Accounting*, Part I, Macmillan.

Nair, R D and Frank, W G (1980) 'The impact of disclosure and measurement practices on international accounting classifications', *Accounting Review*, July.

Nobes, C W (1983) 'A judgmental international classification of financial reporting practices', *Journal of Business Finance and Accounting*, Spring.

Price Waterhouse (1973 and 1975) *Accounting Principles and Reporting Practices* ICAEW, London.

Price Waterhouse (1979) *International Survey of Accounting Principles and Reporting Practices*, Butterworth.

Seidler, L J (1966) 'International accounting – the ultimate theory course', *Accounting Review*, October.

Zeff, S A (1972) *Forging Accounting Principles in Five Countries*, Stipes Publishing, Champaign, Illinois.

CHAPTER 4

EC Harmonisation

4.1 Definition

'Harmonisation' is not an easy word to define. Its arrival in common use in the context of accounting and law seems to be associated with the EC. However, neither the Commission nor other organs of the EC have explicitly defined the word. There seem to be two usages. The most frequently occurring meaning is that two or more systems (of accounting practices or corporate taxation, for example) are made to look more like one another. The rather more subtle alternative meaning is that, without necessarily causing approximation, the systems are made compatible. Some differences can be lived with happily and others cannot be. By analogy, in music it is possible to move discordant notes farther apart and yet make them more harmonious. In practice, harmonisation in accounting tends to mean the process of increasing the compatibility of accounting practices by setting bounds to their degree of variation.

The word 'standardisation' might appear to be stronger; implying the process of making things the same rather than compatible. To some extent, this is true for the accounting standards of the ASC. In some cases these standards proscribe all but one method, and promulgate practice in some detail. However, in many cases, accounting standards merely narrow the range of acceptable practices; this is particularly the case with international standards. Furthermore, whereas the 'harmonisation' proceeding from the EC leads to law, the process of international 'standardisation' encouraged by the International Accounting Standards Committee (IASC) has much less powerful backing. Thus, in accounting, contrary to the general nuances of the words, 'harmonisation' appears to mean something more strict than 'standardisation'. The words themselves and the difference between them are sufficiently vague that it is proposed here to use them in their normal contexts and without the implication of a precise differentiation between them.

4.2 Reasons for Harmonisation

The preparation and products of accounting information are becoming increasingly international. Multinational groups are becoming more dominant and diversifying ever more widely geographically; the holding of shares

38

across national boundaries by persons and (particularly) by institutions is increasingly common, as illustrated by the listing of a growing number of foreign shares and debentures on the New York and London Exchanges; and the multinational accounting firms are constantly expanding their fields of interest and absorbing indigenous firms. These developments increase the practical importance of the differences between accounting systems.

The preceding chapters have discussed the causes of differences in financial reporting in Europe, the nature of those differences, and the way in which the differences may be grouped together. It is clear that, to compilers and interpreters of financial statements from more than one country, these differences are of great significance for the valuation of assets and the measurement of profits. The reasons that make *national* accounting standards desirable also apply internationally. These reasons include the desire to exclude the use of certain misleading practices and to narrow the range of acceptable alternatives so that accounting figures are more comparable between companies. The need for *international* comparability is obvious where shareholders, bankers or revenue authorities operate across national boundaries. Thus, some of the pressure for harmonisation comes from such users. Again, it is not necessary to make accounting rules identical in all relevant countries, but to ensure that they are at least compatible in the sense that, by using information disclosed, useful international comparisons of financial statements can be achieved.

It is not only the various users who might benefit from harmonisation; the compilers and auditors of published financial statements also stand to gain. Further, the differences in accounting are important not only in the context of published financial statements. Because a company's internal accounting system is often heavily influenced by the need to report to shareholders, to governments or to revenue authorities, international differences are also important internally. Such differences lead to problems of performance measurement and investment appraisal within multinational groups.

In summary, the following groups might gain most from European or wider harmonisation of financial reporting:

(*i*) *Investors, investment analysts and stock exchanges*: to enable international comparisons for investment decisions.
(*ii*) *Credit grantors*: for similar reasons to (*i*).
(*iii*) *Multinational companies*: as compilers, investors, appraisers of products or staff, and as staff circulators.
(*iv*) *Multinational accountancy firms*: as auditors and advisers of companies operating in several countries.
(*v*) *Governments*: as tax collectors and controllers of multinationals.

4.3 Factors against Harmonisation

There is a fundamental argument against harmonisation which has been illustrated by the preceding chapters. That is, to the extent that international differences in accounting practices result from underlying economic, legal, social and other environmental factors, harmonisation may not be justified. Different accounting has grown up to serve the different needs of different users; this might suggest that the existing accounting is the 'correct' form for its habitat and should not be changed merely to simplify the work of multinational companies. There does seem to be strength in this point particularly for smaller companies with no significant multinational activities or connections. To foist upon a small private family company in Luxembourg lavish disclosure requirements and the need to report a 'true and fair' view may not be a sensible piece of harmonisation.

The most obvious obstacle to harmonisation is the sheer size and deep-rootedness of the differences in accounting. Even within the 'micro-accounting' or Anglo-Dutch class of countries (see Chapter 3), there are important differences which are difficult to remove. Nevertheless, these pale into insignificance compared to the differences between this class and French or German accounting. As has been discussed, these differences have grown up over the previous century because of differences in users, legal systems and so on. Thus, the differences are structural rather than cosmetic, and require revolutionary action to remove them.

Another facet of this is that professional bodies are strong in Anglo-Dutch countries and weak in continental European countries. This means that it is impossible for professional bodies directly to achieve international harmonisation throughout the developed western world. Thus, although the professional bodies may be able to make some progress in the Anglo-Dutch world, government intervention would be necessary for a wider harmonisation. This brings us to a consideration of the obstacle of nationalism, which may show itself in an unwillingness to accept compromises which involve changing accounting practices towards those of other countries. This unwillingness may be on the part of accountants and companies or on the part of states who may not wish to lose their sovereignty. Another manifestation of nationalism may be the lack of knowledge or interest in accounting elsewhere. A rather more subtle and acceptable variety of this is the concern that it would be difficult to alter internationally set standards in response to a change of mind or a change of circumstances.

Minor difficulties of language, like the French word for both prudence and conservatism being *prudence*, are added to by more complex problems like the translation of 'true and fair'. Particularly in the 1970s, there was considerable incomprehension of this expression in France and Germany, which surfaced most clearly at international conferences.

4.4 Directives and Regulations

The EC achieves its harmonising objectives through two main instruments: Directives, which must be incorporated into the laws of member states; and Regulations, which become law throughout the EC without the need to pass through national legislatures. The concern of this chapter will be with the Directives on company law and with two Regulations. These are listed in Table 4.1 opposite, which also gives a brief description of their scope. The company law Directives of most relevance to accounting are the Fourth and Seventh. These will be discussed in more detail below, after an outline of the procedure for setting Directives.

First, the Commission which is the EC's permanent civil service decides on a project and asks an expert to prepare a report. In the case of the Fourth Directive, this was the Elmendorff Report of 1967. Then an *avant projet* or discussion document is prepared. This is studied by a Commission working party and may lead to the issue of a draft proposed Directive which is

Table 4.1   Directives Relevant to Corporate Accounting

Directives on Company Law	Draft Dates	Date Adopted	Purpose	UK Law
First	1964	1968	Ultra vires rules	1972
Second	1970, 1972	1976	Separation of public companies, minimum capital, distributions	1980
Third	1970, 1973 1975	1978	Mergers	1987
Fourth	1971, 1974	1978	Formats and rules of accounting	1981
Fifth	1972, 1983		Structure and audit of public companies	
Sixth	1975, 1978	1982	De-mergers	1987
Seventh	1976, 1978	1983	Consolidated accounting	1989
Eighth	1978, 1979	1984	Qualifications and work of auditors	1989
Ninth	—		Links between public company groups	
Tenth	1985		International mergers of public companies	
Eleventh	1986		Disclosures relating to branches	
Twelfth	1988		Single member companies	
Vredeling	1980, 1983		Employee information and consultation	
Regulations				
Societas Europea	1970, 1978		European company	
European Economic Interest Grouping	1973, 1978	1985	Joint venture structure	

commented on by the European Parliament (a directly elected assembly with limited powers) and the Economic and Social Committee (a consultative body of employers, employees and others). A revised proposal is then submitted to a Working Party of the Council of Ministers. The Council, consisting of the relevant ministers from each EC country, is the body that adopts a Directive or Regulation. In the case of a Directive, member states are required to introduce a national law within a specified period, though they often exceed it. The Fourth Directive, adopted in June 1978 and notified to member states in July, specified a two-year period followed by up to 18 months for the national law to come into effect. A note on implementation can be found at the end of section 4.6.

Let us take the UK as an example of the enactment of Directives. The First Directive was included in the UK's enabling legislation for entry into the EC in 1972. The requirements of the Second Directive were included in the 1980

41

Companies Act after many additions concerning insider trading, directors duties and several other matters. The Fourth Directive led to the 1981 Companies Act, again with various additions, such as rules on merger accounting and the purchase of own shares. The Third and Sixth Directives (which concern special types of mergers and de-mergers) were implemented by Statutory Instrument in 1987. The Seventh and Eighth Directives were included in the 1989 Companies Act.

4.5 The Second Directive

Of the various matters dealt with by the Second Directive, perhaps the most obvious are the naming of companies, the minimum capital requirements of public companies, and the definition of distributable profit. The first of these was examined in section 1.2 and Table 1.2. As a result of the Second Directive, the UK and Ireland introduced the designation 'public limited company', and the Netherlands introduced the BV as the private limited company.

It has been normal in continental Europe for there to be minimum capital requirements for companies. The Second Directive imposes such a requirement for public companies. The 1980 Act introduced a minimum requirement of £50,000 issued share capital for UK public companies. The Directive contained no requirements for private companies, and none has been introduced in the UK. However, in West Germany the *GmbH Gesetz* (1980) raised the minimum capital requirement of private companies to DM 50,000.

As for the definition of distributable profit, the Directive introduced a definition which in UK law is expressed as: 'accumulated realised profits . . . less . . . accumulated realised losses'. Further, the Directive requires that dividends must not be distributed if they would reduce the net assets below the total of capital and undistributable reserves.

4.6 The Fourth Directive

Survey of Contents

Before examining the effects on particular EC countries, the Fourth Directive itself will be discussed. Article 1 states that the Directive relates to public and private companies throughout the EC, except that member states need not apply the provisions to banks, insurance companies and other financial institutions (for whom a special version of the Fourth Directive was being prepared). Article 2 defines the annual accounts to which it refers as the balance sheet, profit and loss account and notes. Reference to funds flow statements which are standard in the UK and other countries is omitted. The accounts 'shall be drawn up clearly and in accordance with the provisions' of the Directive, except that the need to present a 'true and fair view' may require extra information or may demand a departure from the provisions of the Directive. Such departures must be disclosed. The Directive is intended to establish minimum standards and 'member states may authorise or require' extra disclosure.

Articles 3 to 7 contain general provisions about the consistency and detail of the formats for financial statements. There is a specified order of items, and some items cannot be combined or omitted. Corresponding figures for the previous year must be shown. Articles 8 to 10 detail two formats for balance sheets, one or both of which may be allowed by member states. The Articles allow some combination and omission of immaterial items, but the outline and much detail will be standard.

Articles 11 and 12 allow member states to permit small companies to publish considerably abridged balance sheets. 'Small companies' are those falling below two of the following limits: balance sheet total, 1 million units of account (UA); turnover, 2 million EC units of account; employees, 50. There is also the possibility of lesser reductions for medium-sized companies (see Arts 27 and 47). These size limits are capable of being raised and this happened in 1984. Articles 13 and 14 concern details of disclosure, particularly contingent liabilities, which were shown in the UK but not in some other countries. Articles 15 to 21 concern the definition and disclosure of assets and liabilities. It is useful that 'value adjustments' must be disclosed (Art 15(3)(a)); this will make clearer the conservative revaluations which are common in Franco-German systems.

Articles 22 to 26 specify four formats for profit and loss accounts, which member states may allow companies to choose between. Two of these classify expenses and revenues by nature, and the other two classify them by stage of production. There are two in each case because vertical or two-sided versions may be chosen. Compared with the former sparse UK profit and loss accounts, the disclosure of expenses became very detailed.

However, Art 27 allows member states to permit medium-sized companies to avoid disclosure of the items making up gross profit. In this case original limits were: balance sheet total, 4 million UA; turnover, 8 million UA; employees, 250. Articles 28 to 30 contain some definitions relating to the profit and loss accounts.

Articles 31 and 32 lay out general rules of valuation. The normal Anglo-Dutch principles of accounting are promulgated. Article 33 is a fairly lengthy explanation of the Directive's stance towards accounting for inflation or for specific price changes. Whatever happens, member states must ensure that historical cost information is either shown or can be calculated using notes to the accounts. However, member states may permit or require supplementary or main accounts to be prepared on a replacement value, current purchasing power or other basis. Revaluation of assets would entail a balancing Revaluation Reserve; there are detailed requirements relating to this.

Articles 34 to 42 relate to detailed valuation and disclosure requirements for various balance sheet items. Again the point about the disclosure of 'exceptional value adjustments' is made, this time with specific reference to taxation-induced writings down (Arts 35(1)(d) and 39(e)). The periods over which research and development expenditure and goodwill are written off are to be standardised (Art 37).

Articles 43 to 46 concern the large number of disclosures which will be obligatory in the annual report, including the notes to the accounts. In general, these were already provided in the UK. 'Small companies' (as in Art 11) may be partially exempted. Articles 47 to 51 relate to the audit and publication of accounts. In general, procedures for these matters were allowed to remain as they had been under different national laws. Member states may exempt 'small companies' from publishing profit and loss accounts (Art 47(2)(b)) and from audit (Art 51). This would mean that they would only produce unaudited abridged balance sheets. Article 47(3) allows member states to permit 'medium-sized companies' (as in Art 27) to abridge their balance sheets and notes. However, this abridgement is not as extensive as that for 'small companies', and audit and profit and loss accounts are necessary.

Articles 52 to 62 deal with the implementation of the Directive and with transitional problems, particularly those relating to consolidation, which await the Seventh Directive. A 'Contact Committee' is to be set up to facilitate the application of the Directive and to advise on amendments or additions. Article 55 calls for member states to pass the necessary laws within two years of the July 1978 notification, and then to bring these into force within a further 18 months.

Commentary

The Directive's articles include those referring to valuation rules, formats of published financial statements and disclosure requirements. However, the Directive does not cover the process of consolidation, which is left for the Seventh Directive. As has been mentioned, the EC Commission entrusted the task of preparing the *avant projet* for the Fourth Directive to a working party chaired by a German, Professor Elmendorff. It is not surprising, then, that the first draft of the Directive, published in 1971 (as Table 4.1 records), was based substantially on the German *Aktiengesetz* (Public Companies Act) of 1965. This draft was published before the UK and Ireland entered the EC.

The Directive applies to public and private companies (except for banking, insurance and shipping companies) of all member states. It deals with annual balance sheets and profit and loss accounts, but not with supplementary statements like funds flow statements. The contents of the Directive are discussed below under four headings.

1 Formats

Compared with traditional Anglo-Dutch accounting, perhaps the most obvious feature of the *Aktiengesetz* (*AktG*), and thus of the Fourth Directive, is the prescription of uniform formats. The *AktG*, which was the law for German public companies until 1987 year ends, offered no choice between formats, nor any substantial flexibility within a format. As might have been expected, there was considerable difficulty in arriving at agreed formats for the first draft of the Fourth Directive, even among the six member states belonging to the EC in 1971. This shows itself in the inclusion in the Directive of two balance sheet formats and four profit and loss account formats. These remained largely unaltered in the second draft and the final Directive.

Looking first at the balance sheet, the original German format was reproduced with slight amendment in the 1971 draft of the Fourth Directive (see Table 4.2 opposite). This is a two-sided (or horizontal) balance sheet, with assets on the left. The only significant change between the 1971 draft and those of 1974 and 1978 is in the classification of reserves. The *AktG* and the 1971 draft Directive show profits as the last item on the *credit* side of the balance sheet, and losses as the last item on the *debit* side. Such a treatment of profits fits better with a creditors' or entity view rather than a proprietors' view.

44

Table 4.2   The Evolution of the Balance Sheet (abbreviated versions)

ASSETS shown on left

	AktG (S 151)		1971 Draft (AA 8)		1981 Act (Format 2)
I	Unpaid capital	A	Unpaid capital	A	Unpaid capital
		B	Formation expenses		
II	Fixed and financial	C	Fixed assets	B	Fixed assets
	A Fixed & intangible		I Intangible		I Intangible
			II Tangible		II Tangible
	B Financial		III Participations		III Investments
III	Current assets	D	Current assets	C	Current assets
	A Stocks		I Stocks		I Stocks
	B Other current		II Debtors		II Debtors
			III Securities		III Investments
					IV Cash
IV	Deferred charges	E	Prepayments	D	Prepayments
V	Accumulated losses	F	Loss		
			I For the year		
			II Brought forward		

LIABILITIES AND CAPITAL shown on right

	AktG (S 151)		1971 Draft (AA 8)		1981 Act (Format 2)
I	Share capital	A	Subscribed capital	A	Capital & reserves
II	Disclosed reserves	B	Reserves		I Called up capital
III	Provisions for diminutions	C	Value adjustments		II Share premium
					III Revaluation reserves
					IV Other reserves
					V Profit and loss
IV	Provisions for liabilities	D	Provisions for charges	B	Provisions for L & C
V	Liabilities (4 years +)	E	Creditors	C	Creditors
VI	Other liabilities				
VII	Deferred income	F	Accruals	D	Accruals
VIII	Profit	G	Profit		
			I For the year		
			II Brought forward		

However, in the final Directive, a more Anglo-Dutch approach to reserves is adopted. Format 2 of the 1981 Act (see Table 4.2) follows that of the Directive, except for permitted deletions like formation expenses, which was a necessary heading for practice in some countries. Table 4.2 illustrates the gradual and slight changes in the formats over the 16-year period. It shows only the first two levels of headings. A third level (of sub-sub-headings) is omitted, but in each case does exist and is preceded by Arabic numbers.

Chapter 5 examines the present formats used in several European countries. There it may be seen that harmonisation has not led all balance sheets throughout the EC to look like an expanded version of the format in Table 4.2. There are several reasons why this is not the case. First, the Directive contains another format, as discussed in Chapter 5. Member states were allowed to adopt one format or to permit companies to make the choice as long as they are consistent. The UK and Dutch Acts do the latter, and present the vertical forms as 'Format 1' and 'Format A' respectively, presumably on the grounds that this format corresponds much more closely with previous UK and Dutch practice for published accounts (at least those of large companies). However, the French revised *plan comptable* and the draft German law allow only the horizontal format. The vertical format contains broadly the same headings, sub-headings and sub-sub-headings as the horizontal format, except that current liabilities are shown separately and positioned so as to enable a calculation of net current assets and then net assets.

Secondly, there are several ways in which flexibility is allowed. The *AktG* permitted (i) different classifications for particular trades, (ii) extra detail to be added, and (iii) empty headings to be omitted. The Directive contains these provisions, and also allows Arabic number headings to be combined where the amounts are separately immaterial or where this would lead to greater clarity (in this latter case the information must be shown by note).

Thirdly, more flexibility exists within the Directive's formats than in the *AktG*. This takes the form of several alternative presentations of particular items.

Turning now to the profit and loss account, there is one format only in the *AktG*, but four in each of the versions of the Directive. Member states are allowed to impose particular formats or to allow companies to choose between them. Chapter 5 illustrates how this has been done for some EC countries.

2 Publication and Audit Exemptions

It had long been the practice in many EC countries to exempt all private companies (or small ones) from publication or audit requirements or both. The Directive allows various exemptions for small and medium-sized private companies. Member states may exempt small private companies from drawing up full accounts and from publication of the profit and loss account and from audit. Medium-sized companies may be allowed to draw up abridged profit and loss accounts and not to disclose certain notes. The size criteria and the exemptions adopted in some EC countries are examined in Chapter 5.

3 Accounting 'Principles'

Anglo-Dutch financial reporting has traditionally been free of legal constraints in the area of principles of valuation and measurement, whether from company law, tax law or accounting plan. However, this is far from the case in some other EC countries, especially West Germany whose *Aktiengesetz* was a major source of the Fourth Directive. There are three levels of principle in the *AktG*, in the Directive and in the resulting laws of member states. The first and 'vaguest' level consists of a statement of the overriding purpose of the financial statements. In the *AktG* this was the provisions of the law. By the final 1978 version of the Directive, the overriding purpose had become to give a true and fair view. The evolution of this may be seen in Table 4.3.

Table 4.3   'True and Fair' in the Fourth Directive

1965 Aktiengesetz (S 149)

1   The annual financial statements shall conform to proper accounting principles. They shall be clear and well set out and give as sure a view of the company's financial position and its operating results as is possible pursuant to the valuation provisions.

1971 Draft (Art 2)

1   The annual accounts shall comprise the balance sheet, the profit and loss account and the notes on the accounts. These documents shall constitute a composite whole.

2   The annual accounts shall conform to the principles of regular and proper accounting.

3   They shall be drawn up clearly and, in the context of the provisions regarding the valuation of assets and liabilities and the lay-out of accounts, shall reflect as accurately as possible the company's assets, liabilities, financial position and results.

1974 Draft (Art 2)

1   (As 1971 Draft).

2   The annual accounts shall give a true and fair view of the company's assets, liabilities, financial position and results.

3   They shall be drawn up clearly and in conformity with the provisions of this Directive.

1978 Final (Art 2)

1   (As 1971 Draft).

2   They shall be drawn up clearly and in accordance with the provisions of this Directive.

3   The annual accounts shall give a true and fair view of the company's assets, liabilities, financial position and profit or loss.

4   Where the application of the provisions of this Directive would not be sufficient to give a true and fair view within the meaning of paragraph 3, additional information must be given.

5   Where in exceptional cases the application of a provision of this Directive is incompatible with the obligation laid down in paragraph 3, that provision must be departed from in order to give a true and fair view within the meaning of paragraph 3. Any such departure must be disclosed in the notes on the accounts together with an explanation of the reasons for it and a statement of its effect on the assets, liabilities, financial position and profit or loss. The member states may define the exceptional cases in question and lay down the relevant special rules.

6   The member states may authorise or require the disclosures in the annual accounts of other information as well as that which must be disclosed in accordance with this Directive.

Pressure from the UK, Ireland and the Netherlands had caused its insertion in the 1974 draft and its dominance in the Directive 'in special circumstances'. It should be noted that neither the concept nor the special circumstances need be defined.

The second level of principles has also been substantially affected by Anglo-Dutch accounting. Four accounting conventions found in a British accounting standard, SSAP 2, are enshrined in Art 31 of the Directive: going concern, consistency, prudence and accruals. The first and the last were missing from the first draft of the Directive. However, a fifth principle has been taken from German law, that is the principle that assets and liabilities should be valued separately (for example, when using the lower of cost and net realisable value) before being added together. The concepts were fundamentally acceptable to the Anglo-Dutch view but it was of course a fundamental change of philosophy to find fairly detailed accounting concepts imposed by statute. This change clearly results from the *AktG*.

The third level of principles is more detailed, and, for the UK, Ireland and the Netherlands, involves further encroachment of statute into territory previously regarded as that of the profession. Here, the influence of the *AktG* on the Directive is again clear. In order to enable comparisons within and between industries, to perform meaningful aggregations of companies' accounting figures, and to control the economy, it has seemed appropriate to several continental countries not just to establish uniform formats but to ensure that the items within them are uniformly valued and measured.

The following rules are found in the *AktG* and the Directive:

(*i*)   Fixed assets shall be carried at purchase price or construction cost.
(*ii*) Intangibles may only be shown as assets if acquired for valuable consideration.
(*iii*) Fixed assets with limited useful lives must be depreciated.
(*iv*) The basic rule for valuing current assets is 'lower of cost or net realisable value'.
(*v*)   Current asset valuation may use FIFO, AVCO, LIFO, or similar method.

As with the concepts discussed above, the content of these rules is not out of character for Anglo-Dutch accounting, but their statutory nature was a fundamental change. This has led to several difficulties between law and standards.

Finally, provisions in the Directive allow alternative rules to a strict Germanic historical cost. Departures from historical cost are allowed, ranging from *ad hoc* revaluations of fixed assets to full scale current cost accounting as statutory accounts. Even the first draft of the Directive (before British entry to the EC) allowed for such departures, which would have been necessary to allow for the practice of many Dutch companies. However, the effect is clearly to destroy the attempt to establish uniform accounting measurement rules. Nevertheless, there are important penalties for adopting (or having previously adopted) an alternative to 'Germanic accounting' for any item. These take the form of disclosure requirements, for example in the UK there must be notes concerning:

(*i*)   the valuation basis used,

(*ii*) the comparable historical cost amount or the difference,
(*iii*) the comparable accumulated depreciation under historical cost or the difference,
(*iv*) the revaluation reserve relating to all departures,
(*v*) a note of valuation revisions due to adoption of alternative methods in the year,
(*vi*) the year of valuation,
(*vii*) for assets revalued in the year, the names or qualifications of the valuers.

4   Disclosure Requirements

Disclosure rules are a normal part of any country's statutory requirements. The Fourth Directive includes a large number. Many may be traced to the *AktG* but there are others, such as the requirement to show any effects of tax requirements on accounting numbers, that are an attempt to ensure the provision of information acceptable to those used to Anglo-Dutch accounting.

In several EC countries which had very limited disclosure requirements, the Directive involves major changes.

Implementation

As was mentioned earlier, the Fourth Directive was supposed to be implemented by 1980 and to be in force by 1982. This schedule was not achieved by any country. The dates of implementation are shown in Table 4.4 below. At the time of writing, Italy was being taken to Court by the Commission, but Portugal had transitional relief because of recent accession to the EC. The dates on which the provisions came into force were, of course, after the dates

Table 4.4   Implementation* of Directives

	Fourth	Seventh
Belgium	1985	—
Denmark	1981	—
France	1983	1985
Greece	1987	1987
Luxembourg	1984	1988
Ireland	1986	—
Italy	—	—
Netherlands	1983	1988
Portugal	—	—
Spain	1989	1989
UK	1981	1989
West Germany	1985	1985

*These are the dates of the laws; in many cases there is a considerable delay before they are brought into force.

in Table 4.4. For example, the German law of 1985 was generally to be complied with by 31.12.1987 year-ends.

4.7 The Seventh Directive

This section considers the contents of the Seventh Directive on group accounts. With the Fourth, this is the other major Directive on financial reporting. Drafts of the Directive were published in 1976 and 1978, and the Directive was adopted in 1983. The fact that a Directive on group accounting was adopted as a separate and later Directive from the Fourth is a reminder of the traditional differences in consolidation practices within the EC. British and Dutch accountants might have expected that this issue, which is central for many sets of statutory accounts, would have figured prominently in the EC Commission's plans for rules on financial reporting. Its absence may be explained by the rarity of consolidation in EC member states in the early 1970s. This is discussed in Chapter 2.

The later drafting of the Seventh Directive (subsequent to the accession of the UK, Ireland and Denmark to the EC) helps to explain its Anglo-Dutch, shareholder orientation. The predominance of the Anglo-Dutch view in the 1976 and 1978 drafts became even more noticeable in the adopted Directive of 1983.

Review of Contents

Articles 1–4 require undertakings (which member states may restrict to mean limited companies) to draw up consolidated accounts which include subsidiaries and sub-subsidiaries etc, irrespective of their location. Subsidiaries are defined with respect to majority voting rights or appointment of board members, or dominant influence by contract. However, member states may also require consolidation of companies managed on a unified basis and companies over which a dominant influence is exercised.

Article 5 allows member states to exempt financial holding companies that do not manage their subsidiaries or take part in board appointments. Article 6 allows member states to exempt medium sized and small groups, using the criteria of the Fourth Directive (see Chapter 5) and assuming that no listed company is included. However, until the year 2000, member states may use larger size criteria as specified.

Articles 7 to 11 exempt a company from the requirement to consolidate its own subsidiaries if it is itself a wholly owned subsidiary of an EC company (or a 90% or more owned subsidiary whose minority shareholders approve). However, member states may insist on consolidation by listed subsidiaries. On the other hand, member states may also allow other (less fully owned) subsidiaries not to consolidate unless a certain proportion of shareholders require it. Exemption from consolidation may be linked to a requirement to produce extra information, and the exemption does not necessarily extend to employee reports. Also, member states may exempt further subsidiaries if they are themselves subsidiaries of non-EC parents that prepare suitable consolidated accounts.

Article 12 allows member states to require consolidation where companies are managed on a unified basis or are managed by the same persons.

Articles 13 to 15 allow various subsidiaries to be excluded from consolidation if they are immaterial, if there is severe long-term restriction on assets or management, if there would be disproportionate expense or delay, if they are held for resale, or if their activities are dissimilar (these latter must be excluded if they threaten the true and fair view).

Article 16 requires that consolidated accounts shall be clear and shall give a true and fair view. Article 17 requires the Fourth Directive's formats to be used, suitably amended. Article 18 requires consolidation to be 100%. Article 19 requires there to be a once-and-for-all calculation of goodwill based on fair values at the date of first consolidation or at the date of purchase.

Article 20 allows merger accounting where any cash payment represents less than 10% of the nominal value of the shares issued. Articles 21–23 require minority interests to be shown separately, and 100% of income of consolidated companies to be included. Articles 24–28 require consistency, elimination of intra-group items, use of the parent's year end as the group's year-end (normally), and disclosure of information to enable meaningful temporal comparisons where the composition of the group has changed.

Article 29 requires the valuation rules of the Fourth Directive to be used, and uniform rules to be used for the consolidation of all subsidiaries. There must be disclosure of differences between parent and group practices. Tax-based valuations must be 'corrected' (or member states may allow them merely to be disclosed) in the consolidation.

Articles 30–31 require positive goodwill on consolidation to be depreciated or to be immediately writen off against reserves, and negative goodwill only to be taken to profit if it is realised or where it was due to the expectation of future costs or losses.

Article 32 allows member states to require or permit proportional consolidation for joint ventures. Article 33 requires associated companies to be recorded as a single item, initially valued at cost or at the proportion of net assets. Subsequently, the appropriate share of profits must be included in the group accounts.

Articles 34 to 36 call for a large number of disclosures relating to group companies and consolidation methods. Articles 37 and 38 deal with publication and audit. Articles 39 to 51 deal with transitional and enabling provisions.

Commentary

The 1976 and 1978 drafts of the Directive contained many more elements of continental European practice than does the adopted version described above. For example, *de facto* rather than *de jure* control was the criterion for consolidation; consolidation was required even where the head of the group was not a company; and EC level consolidations ('horizontal consolidations') were required when the head of the company was registered outside the EC. These three ideas remain in the Directive but they are now options.

The resulting Directive is very close to UK practice in its main provisions. As an illustration of this, some main provisions are listed in Table 4.5 overleaf, showing which countries' pre-Directive practices they accord closest with. In addition, some of the options are examined in the same way in Table 4.6 overleaf.

Clearly great changes were or are in store for countries other than the UK,

Table 4.5   Main Provisions of Seventh Directive

		Source Countries
Art 1	Subsidiaries defined principally in terms of *de jure* criteria	UK, IRL
Art 3	Consolidation to include foreign subsidiaries	UK, IRL, NL, F
Art 4	Consolidation irrespective of legal form of subsidiary	WG
Art 4	Consolidation by all types of companies	UK, IRL, NL
Art 7	Exemption from preparation of group accounts by wholly-owned subsidiaries	UK, IRL, NL, F
Art 16	True and fair view	UK, IRL, NL
Art 17	Uniform formats to be used	WG, F
Art 19	Goodwill to be calculated once-for-all	UK, IRL, NL, F
Art 19	Goodwill to be based on fair values	UK, IRL, NL
Art 29	Tax-based valuations to be 'corrected' or at least disclosed	UK, IRL, NL
Art 30	Goodwill to be depreciated or written off	UK, IRL, NL, F
Art 33	Equity method for associated companies	UK, IRL, NL, F

Table 4.6   Options in the Seventh Directive

		Source Countries
Arts 1, 12	Group companies to include those managed on a unified basis or dominantly influenced	NL, WG
Art 4	Requirements to consolidate may be restricted to parents that are companies	UK, IRL
Art 5	Financial holding companies may be exempted	Lux
Art 6	Consolidation may be restricted to 'large' groups	approx F, WG
Art 11	Groups exempted if owned by non-EC parents that prepare suitable accounts	UK, IRL, NL
Art 13	Exclusion on basis of immateriality, long-term restrictions, expense or delay	UK, IRL, NL, F
Art 20	Merger accounting allowed	UK, IRL
Art 32	Proportional consolidation allowed	F, NL

Ireland and the Netherlands. The most noticeable changes in Germany are the extension of consolidation to more groups, the inclusion of associated companies and foreign subsidiaries, and a new method of calculating differences arising on consolidation. In France, the most obvious changes are extension of the rules beyond listed companies and the imposition of greater uniformity. In Italy, Greece, Portugal, Spain and Luxembourg consolidation will cease to be a great rarity.

Implementation

The Seventh Directive was intended to be implemented throughout the EC by 1 January 1988 (except for delays allowed for Greece, Spain and Portugal). Although France and West Germany were slow to enact the Fourth Directive, they have been the leaders with the Seventh: in January 1985 (partially) and in December 1985, respectively. Some implementation dates are shown in Table 4.4.

Many options still remain in the Directive and, at the time of writing, several countries have not decided precisely how to implement it. Chapter 8 examines the consolidation practice of several European countries in more detail. As an example of differences, Table 8.3 shows the implementation (or proposed implementation) of certain aspects of the definition of a subsidiary.

CHAPTER 5

Publication and Audit of Accounts

5.1 Introduction

Because of the importance of 'outsiders' as providers of finance in the UK, Ireland and the Netherlands, there has been a long tradition of voluntary publication and audit of annual accounts. This has been increasingly overtaken in the second half of the twentieth century by the appearance of guidelines or standards from the accountancy profession and of company laws. At one extreme, the UK has required publication and audit for all limited companies (nearly a million). At the other extreme, publication and audit has been rare in Switzerland and most Mediterranean countries. Even in West Germany, until the late 1980s, publication and audit were restricted to a few thousand large and public companies.

As has been discussed in the previous chapter, the EC Fourth Directive allows member states to exempt small companies from audit and from the publication of profit and loss accounts. Some exemptions are also allowed for medium-sized companies. The size definitions are expressed in the Fourth Directive in European currency units (ecu), above which member states may not go. Some examples of member state interpretations of this are shown in Table 5.1 opposite. A company must fall below two of the three thresholds in order to qualify.

Because there are options in the Directive and because member states can always be more severe than the Directive requires, the national laws are different. For example, the UK does not exempt small companies from audit, whereas West Germany does. Although the Directive led to a massive extension of audit for Germany, most companies are still exempted because most companies are 'small'. Table 5.2 opposite summarises some of the provisions for four countries.

Italy, Spain and Portugal had not brought the Directive into force in the 1980s, so publication and audit remained rare, largely restricted to listed companies or even less. This is also the situation for Switzerland.

Furthermore, apart from in the UK, Ireland and the Netherlands, supplementary information is also rare in Europe. For example, most countries do not require the publication of funds flow statements, interim reports or earnings per share information. In those cases where companies volunteer to produce such information, there is a lack of rules and therefore a lack of reliability and consistency.

54

Table 5.1   Size Criteria in Four European Countries

For small companies:

	UK	**Netherlands**
Turnover:	£2 million	fl 8 million
Balance sheet total:	£0.975	fl 4 million
Employees:	50	50
	France	**West Germany**
Turnover:	FF 3 million	DM 8 million
Balance sheet total:	FF 1.5 million	DM 3.9 million
Employees:	10	50

For medium-sized companies:

	UK	**Netherlands**
Turnover:	£8 million	fl 35 million
Balance sheet total:	£3.9 million	fl 17 million
Employees:	250	250
	France	**West Germany**
Turnover:	FF 20 million	DM 32 million
Balance sheet total:	FF 10 million	DM 15.5 million
Employees:	50	250

Table 5.2   Exemptions in Four European Countries

The exemptions from publication and audit are as follows for small companies:

UK	**Netherlands**
Exemption from publication (though not from audit and sending to shareholders) of profit and loss account, directors' report and many notes; and balance sheet abbreviated.	Abbreviated formats for statements. Also, exempt from audit.
France	**West Germany**
Abridged accounts and notes may be published.	Exempt from audit.

For medium-sized companies:

UK	Netherlands
Abbreviated profit and loss account (for publication purposes only).	Abbreviated profit and loss account.
France	**West Germany**
Abridged notes in published accounts.	May be audited by Vereidigte Buchprüfer rather than by Wirtschaftsprüfer.

5.2 Formats

Uniform formats are originally a German idea, but one now adopted elsewhere; for example, through the accounting plans of France, Spain and Greece. As discussed in the previous chapter, the Fourth Directive imposes uniform formats, but with some flexibility. Table 5.3 below shows how some member states have chosen formats. For France there is greater flexibility than shown here in the case of group accounts. The 'gross profit' and 'total output' versions of the profit and loss account can be seen in the Appendix to this chapter, for example, in the UK formats 1 and 2. The German company's format in Table 2.1 is a 'total output' version.

Table 5.3   Format Types in Four European Countries

	UK	Netherlands
Balance sheet:	Both allowed. Vertical normal.	Both allowed. Vertical normal.
Profit & loss:	All allowed. Vertical normal. 'Gross profit' most usual.	All allowed. Vertical normal.
	France	**West Germany**
Balance sheet:	Two-sided only.	Two-sided only.
Profit & loss:	'Total output' formats only. Vertical normal in group accounts.	Vertical only. 'Total output' normal.

5.3 Terminology

Naturally, language is a major difficulty when dealing with European financial statements. Not only must the analyst master technical accounting terms but foreign languages also. Many large continental European companies publish versions of their accounts in English (or 'American'). However, many do not.

Even accounts in English may have unreliable or misleading translations and, at worst, the English version may be little more than a marketing document. Such versions are, of course, not the real statutory accounts, nor do they have to obey UK rules, so they may be extracts or manipulations of the original.

Some examples of translation problems will help to illustrate these points. The accounts of Total Oil (for France) and AEG (for Germany) continue to be used for this purpose. Full versions of the accounts of these companies can be found in appendices at the end of this book. There is no suggestion that these companies are worse than any others, indeed they are better than many; it is merely that language is a complex problem in a technical area like accounting.

Example 1
The following is an extract from the English-version annual report of Total Oil:
'Foreign currency balance sheets are converted into French francs on the basis of exchange rates at 31 December 1987. The conversion is applied to fixed assets as well as to monetary assets and liabilities. Gains or losses on translation of their balance sheets at the end of the previous year are dealt with . . .'.

This extract shows the word 'conversion' being used interchangeably with 'translation' because the two accounting terms are the same in French (*conversion*). In English the former means a physical act of exchange, whereas the latter (which would be correct here) means an accounting manipulation.

Example 2
A further extract, as found in earlier years of Total Oil reports:
'However, as concerns newly acquired companies the excess of the TOTAL Group's investment in such companies . . . is capitalized in the consolidated balance sheet and is not amortized. . . . These surplus values are depreciated on a straightline basis . . .'.

The expression 'surplus values' is a translation of *survaleurs*. The English accounting expression would have been 'goodwill'.

Example 3
Appendix II (p 140) shows one of the balance sheets of the 1988 AEG report. As may be seen, the translation is into 'American'; for example 'inventories' and 'trade receivables'. More interestingly, the title states 'Consolidated Balance Sheet of AEG Aktiengesellschaft'. Yet, several factors prove that it is actually the parent company's *unconsolidated* balance sheet:

(*i*)   It states 'AEG Aktiengesellschaft'; that is, a company not a group.
(*ii*)   If this is not the parent's balance sheet, then there is not one in the annual report, as there should be.
(*iii*) The figure for 'financial assets' is very large; it is of course the shares in the subsidiaries at cost.
(*iv*)   There are no minority interests shown.

In other words, although the document states that it is consolidated, it is not: a form of translation problem.

Example 4
When matters get complicated, a translation often becomes opaque. AEG's note

on consolidated techniques is very difficult to understand. It is shown in Table 5.4 with the present author's interpretation. The technical points are discussed further in Chapter 8.

The general problem illustrated by these examples is that, although the language may be of good quality, the translation is often not done by accountants, perhaps because bilingual accountants are very expensive to hire. For example, there are no such terms in British accounting as 'surplus values' (Example 2) or 'capital consolidation' or 'book value method' (Example 4). Of course, none of this should be read as implying a lack of gratitude for translations: it is a very rare US or UK company that bothers at all.

In order to help the reader as far as possible in cases where there is no translation, there is a four-language glossary of terms at the end of this book. An Anglo-American comparison and a detailed explanation of terms can be found in the companion volume, *Interpreting US Financial Statements*.

---

*Table 5.4   Illustration of Language Problems**

Original	**Author's Interpretation**
Capital consolidation is performed using the 'book value method'. Under this method, the book values of the affiliated companies are netted against the underlying equity in these companies at the time of acquisition or initial consolidation.	Full consolidation is performed using a version of fair value accounting. Under this method, the first stage is to compare the cost of the consolidated companies with the book value of the group's share of their net assets. Generally this is done at the date of acquisition, but for existing subsidiaries that have been consolidated for the first time this year, the year end values are used.
Where the book values exceed underlying equity, the difference is allocated to the respective assets or liabilities according to their real value. A difference remaining after the allocation is shown as goodwill or disclosed as a reduction from the reserves. If the book values fall below the underlying equity, the difference is recorded as 'reserve arising from consolidation'.	Where cost exceeds net assets, the difference is allocated to the subsidiary's assets and liabilities up to and in proportion to their fair values. Any excess remaining is goodwill, which is either shown as an asset or written off against reserves.
	Where the initial exercise leads to a negative difference, this is shown as a 'reserve arising from consolidation'.

*The original is from AEG's published translation of its 1987 Accounts.

Appendix to Chapter 5: Formats

The compulsory or the most frequently found formats for financial statements are shown in the following pages. The lowest level of detail in the formats may generally be disclosed in the notes, so that published accounts do not look exactly as shown in this appendix.

The formats shown here are, in order of appearance:

1   **UK.** The vertical balance sheet used by the great majority of companies.

2   **UK.** The most frequently used profit and loss account.

3   **UK.** The minority-used profit and loss account.

4   **Netherlands.** The vertical balance sheet used by many large companies.

5, 6 **Netherlands.** The two most used profit and loss account formats.

7   **France.** The balance sheet (for individual companies).

8   **France.** The two-sided profit and loss account.

9   **West Germany.** The balance sheet.

10   **West Germany.** The more normal profit and loss account.

11   **West Germany.** The optional profit and loss account.

1

UK, Balance Sheet, Format 1 (presented vertically)

Called up share capital not paid

Fixed assets

Intangible assets
  Development costs
  Concessions, patents, licences, trade
    marks and similar rights and assets
  Goodwill
  Payments on account

Tangible assets
  Land and buildings
  Plant and machinery
  Fixtures, fittings, tools and
    equipment
  Payments on account and assets in
    course of construction

Investments

  Shares in group companies
  Loans to group companies
  Interests in associated undertakings
  Other participating interests
  Other investments other than loans
  Other loans
  Own shares

Current assets

Stocks
  Raw materials and consumables
  Work in progress
  Finished goods and goods for resale
  Payments on account

Debtors
  Trade debtors
  Amounts owed by group companies
  Amounts owed by related companies
  Other debtors
  Called up share capital not paid
  Prepayments and accrued income

Investments
  Shares in group companies
  Own shares
  Other investments

Cash at bank and in hand

Prepayments and accrued income

*Creditors: amounts falling due within
one year*
  Debenture loans
  Bank loans and overdrafts
  Payments received on account
  Trade creditors
  Bills of exchange payable
  Amounts owed to group companies
  Amounts owed to related companies
  Other creditors including taxation
    and social security
  Accruals and deferred income

Net current assets (liabilities)

Total assets less current liabilities

*Creditors: amounts falling due after
more than one year*

Debenture loans
  Bank loans and overdrafts
  Payments received on account
  Trade creditors
  Bills of exchange payable
  Amounts owed to group companies
  Amounts owed to related companies
  Other creditors including taxation
    and social security
  Accruals and deferred income

Provisions for liabilities and charges
  Pensions and similar obligations
  Taxation, including deferred taxation
  Other provisions

Accruals and deferred income

Minority interests

Capital and reserves

Called up share capital

Share premium account

Revaluation reserve

Other reserves
  Capital redemption reserve
  Reserve for own shares
  Reserves provided for and by the
    articles of association
  Other reserves
Profit and loss account

2

UK, Profit and Loss Account, Format 1

Turnover
Cost of sales
Gross profit or loss
Distribution costs
Administrative expenses
Other operating income
Income from interests in associated undertakings
Income from other participating interests
Income from other fixed asset investments
Other interest receivable and similar income
Amounts written off investments
Interest payable and similar charges
Profit or loss on ordinary activities before tax
Tax on profit or loss on ordinary activities
Profit or loss on ordinary activities after taxation
Profit or loss on ordinary activities attributable to minority interests
Extraordinary income
Extraordinary charges
Extraordinary profit or loss
Tax on extraordinary profit or loss
Profit or loss on extraordinary activities attributable to minority interests
Other taxes not shown under the above items
Profit or loss for the financial year

3

UK, Profit and Loss Account, Format 2

Turnover
Change in stocks of finished goods and in work in progress
Own work capitalised
Other operating income
Raw materials and consumables
Other external charges
Staff costs:
(*a*) wages and salaries
(*b*) social security costs
(*c*) other pension costs
Depreciation and other amounts written off tangible and intangible fixed
  assets
Exceptional amounts written off current assets
Other operating charges
Income from shares in group companies
Income from shares in related companies
Income from other fixed asset investments
Amounts written off investments
Interest payable and similar charges
Profit or loss on ordinary activities before tax
Tax on profit or loss on ordinary activities
Profit or loss on ordinary activities after taxation
Profit or loss on ordinary activities attributable to minority interests
Extraordinary income
Extraordinary charges
Extraordinary profit or loss
Profit or loss on ordinary activities before tax
Tax on extraordinary profit or loss
Profit or loss on extraordinary activities attributable to minority interests
Other taxes not shown under the above items
Profit or loss for the financial year

4

Netherlands, Balance Sheet, Format A

Balance sheet as at

Fixed assets

Intangible fixed assets
  share issue expenses
  research and development
  concessions and licences
  intellectual property rights
  goodwill
  payments on account

Tangible fixed assets
  land and buildings
  plant and machinery
  fixtures, fittings, tools and equipment
  in the course of construction and
    payments on account
  not employed in the production process

Fixed asset investments
  group companies
  amounts owed by group companies
  other participating interests
  amounts owed by related companies
  other investments
  other loans

Total fixed assets

Current assets

Stocks
  raw materials and consumables
  work in progress
  finished goods and goods for sale
  payments on account

Debtors
  trade debtors
  amounts owed by group companies
  amounts owed by related companies
  other debtors
  called up share capital not paid
  prepayments and accrued income

Investments
  shares, or depositary receipts thereof, in
  group companies
  other investments

Cash at bank, giro and in hand

Total current assets

Current liabilities

Creditors due within one year
  convertible debentures and other loans
  other debentures and private loans
  amounts owed to credit institutions
  advance payments received on orders
  trade creditors and trade credits
  bills of exchange and cheques payable
  amounts owed to group companies
  amounts owed to related companies
  taxation and social security
  pensions
  other creditors
  accruals and deferred income

Net current assets

Total assets less current liabilities

Long-term liabilities

Creditors due after more than one year
  convertible debentures and other loans
  other debentures and private loans
  amounts owed to credit institutions
  advance payments received on orders
  trade creditors and trade credits
  bills of exchange and cheques payable
  amounts owed to group companies
  amounts owed to related companies
  taxation and social security
  pensions
  other creditors
  accruals and deferred income

Provisions for liabilities and charges

  pensions
  taxation
  other

Capital and reserves

Paid up and called up share capital

Share premium account

Revaluation reserve

*Statutory reserves and articles of
association reserves*
  statutory reserves
  articles of association reserves

Other reserves

Undistributed profit

63

5

Netherlands, Profit and Loss Account, Format E

Net turnover

Change in stocks of finished goods and work in progress
Own work capitalised
Other operating income

Total operating income

Raw materials
Work contracted out and other external expenses
Salaries and wages
Social security
Amortisation, depreciation and diminution in value of intangible and
Tangible fixed assets
Exceptional diminution in value of current assets
Other operating expenses

Total operating expenses

Operating profit or loss

Profit or loss on fixed asset investments
Other interest receivable and similar income
Profit or loss on participating interests
Increase in value of remaining fixed asset investments and current invest-
ments
Decrease in value of remaining fixed asset investments and current
Investments
Interest payable and similar expenses

Balance of financial income and expense

Profit or loss on ordinary activities before taxation

Tax on profit or loss on ordinary activities

Profit or loss on ordinary activities after taxation

Extraordinary income
Extraordinary expense

Extraordinary profit or loss before taxation

Tax on extraordinary profit or loss

Extraordinary profit or loss after taxation

Profit or loss after taxation

6

Netherlands, Profit and Loss Account, Format F

Net turnover

    Cost of sales

Gross margin on turnover

    Distribution expenses
    General administrative expenses

Total expenses

Net margin on turnover

    Other operating income

Operating profit and loss

    Profit or loss on fixed asset investments
    Other interest receivable and similar income
    Profit or loss on participating interests
    Increase in value of remaining fixed asset investments and current investments
    Decrease in value of remaining fixed asset investments and current investments
    Interest payable and similar expenses

Balance of financial income and expense

Profit or loss on ordinary activities before taxation

    Tax on profit or loss on ordinary activities

Profit or loss on ordinary activities after taxation

    Extraordinary income
    Extraordinary expense

Extraordinary profit or loss before taxation

Profit or loss after taxation

7

France, Balance Sheet

Assets	**Capital and liabilities**
Issued share capital not called	

Assets

Issued share capital not called

Fixed Assets
 Intangible fixed assets
  Formation costs
  Research and development costs
  Concessions, patents, licences,
   trademarks, and similar rights and
   assets
  Goodwill
  Other intangible fixed assets
  Payments on account

 Tangible fixed assets
  Land
  Buildings
  Plant, machinery, tools
  Other tangible fixed assets
  Tangible fixed assets in course of
   construction
  Payments on account

 Investments
  Shares in group and related
   companies
  Amounts owed by group and related
   companies
  Other fixed asset investments
  Other loans
  Other investments

Current Assets
 Stocks and work in progress
 Raw materials and consumables
 Work in progress (goods & services)
 Intermediate and finished goods
 Goods for resale

 Payments on account and deposits

 Debtors
  Trade debtors
  Other debtors
  Called up share capital not paid

 Investments
  Own shares
  Other investments

 Cash at bank and in hand

Prepayments and Accrued Income
 Prepayments
 Accrued income

Debenture redemption premiums

Translation differences

Capital and liabilities

Capital and Reserves
 Share capital (of which paid up . . .)
 Share premiums
 Revaluation reserves
 Reserves:
  Legal reserve
  Reserves required by articles or by
   contract
  Reserves required by regulations
  Other (optional) reserves
 Carry forward from profit and loss
  account
  (credit or debit balance)
  Profit or loss for the accounting
   period

Sub-total: Net worth

Investment subsidies
Provisions required by regulations

Provisions for Liabilities and Charges
 Provisions for liabilities
 Provisions for charges

Creditors
 Convertible debenture loans
 Other debenture loans
 Loans and sundry creditors
 Payments received on account
 Trade creditors
 Debts relating to fixed assets
 Taxation and social security
 Other creditors
 Accruals and deferred income

Translation differences

8

France, Profit and Loss Account, Two-sided Version

Expenses	**Income**

Operating expenses
  Purchases of goods for resale
    Variation in stocks thereof
  Purchases of raw materials and
    consumables
    Variation in stocks thereof
  Other purchases and external charges
  Taxes and similar payments
  Wages and salaries
  Social security costs
  Valuation adjustments
    on fixed assets: depreciation
    on fixed assets: other amounts
      written off
    on current assets: amounts written
      off
    relating to provisions for liabilities
      and charges
  Other operating expenses

          TOTAL operating expenses

Share of loss on joint ventures

Financial expenses
  Value adjustments
  Interest and similar expenses
  Losses on foreign exchange
  Net loss on transfers of short-term
    securities

          TOTAL financial expenses

Exceptional expenses
  Operating
  Non-operating
  Depreciation and other amounts
    written off

          TOTAL exceptional expenses

Profit share of employees

Tax on profit

          TOTAL expenses

  Balance–profit

          SUM TOTAL

Operating income
  Sales of goods bought for resale
  Sales of goods and services produced
    Net turnover
    (including exports)
  Variation in stock of finished goods
    and work in progress
  Work performed for own purposes
    and capitalised
  Operating subsidies
  Provisions written back
  Other operating income

          TOTAL operating income

Share of profit on joint ventures

Financial income
  From participating interests
  From other investments and loans
    forming part of the fixed assets
  Other interest receivable and similar
    income
  Provisions written back
  Gains on foreign exchange
  Net gain from transfers of short-term
    securities

          TOTAL financial income

Exceptional income
  Operating
  Non-operating
  Provisions written back

          TOTAL exceptional income

          TOTAL income

  Balance–loss

          SUM TOTAL

67

9

West Germany, Balance Sheet

Fixed assets

Intangible assets
Concessions, industrial and similar
rights and assets and licences in
such rights and assets;
Goodwill
Payments on account

Tangible assets
Land, land rights and buildings
including buildings on third party
land
Technical equipment and machines
Other equipment, factory and office
equipment
Payments on account and assets
under construction

Financial assets
Shares in affiliated enterprises
Loans to affiliated enterprises
Participations
Loans to enterprises in which
participations are held
Long-term investments
Other loans

Current Assets

Inventories
Raw materials and supplies
Work in process
Finished goods and merchandise
Payments on account

Receivables and other assets
Trade receivables
Receivables from affiliated enterprises
Receivables from enterprises in which
participations are held
Other assets

Securities
Shares in affiliated enterprises
Own shares
Other securities

Cheques, cash-in-hand, central bank
and postal giro balances, bank
balances

Prepaid

Equity

Subscribed capital
Capital reserves
Revenue reserves
Legal reserve
Reserve for own shares
Statutory reserves
Other revenue reserves

Retained profits/accumulated losses
brought forward

Net income/net loss for the year

Accruals

Accruals for pensions and similar
obligations
Tax accruals
Other accruals

Liabilities

Loans
of which convertible:
Liabilities to banks
Payments received on account of orders
Trade payables
Liabilities on bills accepted and drawn
Payable to affiliated enterprises
Payable to enterprises in which
participations are held
Other liabilities,
of which taxes:
of which relating to social security
and similar obligations:

Deferred income

10

West Germany, Profit and Loss Account, First Format

Sales

Increase or decrease in finished goods inventories and work in process

Own work capitalised

Other operating income

Cost of materials:

    Cost of raw materials, consumables and supplied and of purchased merchandise

    Cost of purchased services

Personnel expenses:

    Wages and salaries

    Social security and other pension costs,

        of which in respect of old age pensions:

Depreciation:

    On intangible fixed assets and tangible assets as well as on capitalised start-up and business expansion expenses

    On current assets to the extent that it exceeds depreciation which is normal for the company

Other operating expenses

Income from participations,

of which from affiliated enterprises:

Income from other investments and long-term loans,

    of which relating to affiliated enterprises;

Other interest and similar income,

    of which from affiliated enterprises:

Amortisation of financial assets and investments classified as current assets

Interest and similar expenses,

    of which to affiliated enterprises:

Results from ordinary activities

Extraordinary income

Extraordinary expense

Extraordinary results

Taxes on income

Other taxes

Net income/net loss for the year

11

West Germany, Profit and Loss Account, Second Format

Sales
Cost of sales
Gross profit on sales
Selling expenses
General administration expenses
Other administration expenses
Other operating income
Other operating expenses
Income from participations,
    of which from affiliated enterprises:
Income from other investments and financial assets,
    of which from affiliated enterprises:
Other interest and similar income,
    of which from affiliated enterprises:
Amortisation of financial assets and investments classified as current assets
Interest and similar expenses
    of which to affiliated enterprises:
Results from ordinary activities
Extraordinary income
Extraordinary expense
Extraordinary results
Taxes on income
Other taxes
Net income/net loss for the year

CHAPTER 6

The Valuation of Assets

This chapter looks at some major European differences in the methods for valuing assets in the balance sheets of companies. This is a vital matter because it directly affects the calculation of totals such as net assets, total assets, shareholders' funds, total capital, and so on. In order to assess the profitability of one company in comparison with another, at least one of these aggregate measures will be necessary. Given that assets are valued differently, international comparisons lack much meaning unless some adjustment is made for this.

The differences discussed in this chapter exist despite the first round of harmonisation of accounting in the EC, caused by the Fourth Directive on company law. In order to get international agreement, the Directive had to contain compromises and options. This is particularly obvious in the area of asset valuation, where many alternatives exist for member states. Most of the variety shown below will continue to exist in 1992 and beyond.

Topics which are more closely related to the measurement of profit are dealt with in Chapter 7. The inter-related matters of consolidation, currency translation and segmental reporting are left for Chapter 8. Readers are directed to Appendices I and II for a full reproduction of French and German notes on asset valuations.

6.1 Tangible Fixed Assets

It is easier to put a reliable value on tangible fixed assets (such as land, buildings or machines) than on intangibles (such as patents, licences or trade marks). Nevertheless, there are still many ways in which valuation can be done, and predominant practice differs country by country across Europe.

Section 2.5 used tangible fixed assets as an example of valuation differences, and the discussion there can serve as an introduction. It is pointed out there that historical cost is the traditional method of asset valuation in most countries. Some European countries are looked at in more detail below:

(*i*)   *Germany*:   Strict historical cost, except for write-downs for depreciation and other tax-allowed reductions. This latter point applies to most countries and will not be repeated.

France: Historical cost, except that assets were revalued in 1978 at 1976 values in a tax-exempt way, subsequent depreciation being based on these values (see box below). For group accounts, valuations can move away from these tax-controlled numbers.

---

1 VALUATION OF FIXED ASSETS (France, Total Oil, 1987)

'Fixed Assets—1976 Revaluation

Gross fixed assets of the French companies are included in the consolidated balance sheet at their book values. Fixed assets revalued by these companies in **1978** are accordingly included at their revised value.

In order to ensure consistency in the revaluation of Group assets, revaluations carried out by the foreign subsidiaries (but not incorporated in their own accounts), which are based upon the methods used by the French companies, have been included in the consolidated balance sheet.'

(*iii*) *Italy, Spain*: Somewhat similar to France, with tax-induced revaluations in the 1980s.

(*iv*) *Switzerland*: Historical cost, except that consolidated accounts are not compulsory so that no valuation rules apply. For example, Ciba-Geigy have been using current cost in their group accounts (see box below).

CURRENT VALUE (Switzerland, Ciba-Geigy)

'In the Summary of Financial Results, both sales on the one hand and expenses and costs on the other are stated at current value. Depreciation at current value assists in the maintenance of physical capital, and the appearance of paper profits in the accounts is avoided.

The current value principle is applied to the Summary of Financial Status by means of adjustments to the fixed assets and revaluation of stocks.'

(*v*) *Sweden*: Historical cost.

(*vi*) *UK, Ireland*: Historical cost, or current cost or market value (need not be current). Valuations can be, and for large companies often are, done on an *ad hoc* basis. However, there must be disclosure of the basis of valuation and what the historical cost would have been.

(*vii*) *Netherlands*: Somewhat like the UK, except that some companies use replacement cost as the main basis of valuation.

Chapters 1 and 2 examine the effect of taxation on asset valuation in most continental countries. This can lead to valuations which are far removed from commercial reality.

The Fourth Directive requires the disclosure of valuations that are determined by tax rules rather than by commercial or company law provisions. It is becoming increasingly easy to detect major instances of this, as the following German example shows:

DISCLOSURE OF TAX-BASED VALUATIONS (Germany, Henkel)

'In the financial statements of Henkel KGaA at December 31, 1987, all differences between valuations allowable under company law regulations and valuations made solely in accordance with tax regulations are shown as special accounts with reserve element. In the consolidated financial statements these special accounts are added to revenue reserves, after allowing for deferred taxation at the average rate chargeable on profits of the Group.'

A particular quirk of the UK and Ireland is that the relevant accounting standard (SSAP 19) requires investment properties to be annually revalued and not to be subject to systematic depreciation. In other countries investment properties are not treated differently from other properties.

6.2 Intangible Assets

Practice in this area varies greatly from country to country, and within a country. Goodwill on consolidation is a particular problem which is left for Chapter 8.

For example, in Germany it was normal until the end of 1987 (when the EC Fourth Directive came into force) to write many intangible assets off to zero on purchase (see box below). This is still possible outside the EC. At the other extreme, in the late 1980s, some UK companies began to value and capitalise internally developed brand names. The valuation method appears to be current cost, which is legal.

---

2 INTANGIBLES (Germany, AEG)

'Under the *intangible assets*, patents and similar rights acquired in 1987 are valued for the first time at cost, less scheduled amortization' (ie they were valued at zero before).

In general, however, intangible assets are valued, like other fixed assets, at historical cost less depreciation.

Under certain conditions, development expenditure can be capitalised and written off over its useful economic life in some countries (eg UK, France, Sweden, Spain and the Netherlands) but cannot be in others (eg Germany). Formation expenses may be capitalised and written off over five years in France, Germany, the Netherlands and Spain, but must not be capitalised in the UK and Ireland.

6.3 Stocks (Inventories)

The 'lower of cost and market' rule is used throughout Europe, as a means of ensuring the prudent valuation of stock. It is required by the EC Fourth Directive. In most countries 'market' means net realisable value, but it can mean other valuations; for example, in Germany and Spain, replacement cost would be used where this is even lower than historical cost or net realisable value (see box below). In the Netherlands some companies value at the lower of replacement cost and net realisable value.

Stocks (Spain, Union Explosivos)

'Stocks are valued at cost which is less than replacement cost or net realizable value. The criteria used in establishing cost are as follows:
Materials and supplies:
    At purchase cost calculated on a first-in, first-out basis.
Work-in-progress and finished goods:
    At manufactured cost calculated on a first-in, first-out basis, including materials and supplies, direct and indirect labour costs, depreciation and other related manufacturing charges.'

The determination of cost may involve the use of FIFO (first in, first out), LIFO (last in, first out), weighted average or some other method. In the UK, Ireland, France and Sweden, LIFO is not allowed for tax or accounting purposes. In Germany and Spain, LIFO is allowed where it corresponds to physical usage. In the Netherlands, LIFO is allowed but unusual. The treatment of overheads can vary. In most countries, only production overheads are included, but in Germany and Sweden the appropriate proportion of administration overheads may also be included.

Long-term contracts are accounted for on the percentage-of-completion method in the UK, Ireland and the Netherlands; this allows a proportion of profit to be taken as production proceeds. By contrast, the recording of profit usually waits for completion in France, Germany and Sweden.

6.4 Debtors

As a result of prudence, debtors are valued in all countries with reference to future expected receipts rather than to legal obligations outstanding. Specific and general provisions for doubtful debts are deducted from debtors and charged as expenses. For countries within the EC, the Fourth Directive requires separate disclosure of any amounts included under debtors (and therefore under 'current assets') that are not expected to be received within a year from the balance sheet date.

In some countries, such as Germany and Italy, there may be a tendency to increase general provisions because these are tax deductible. Also, in some countries, such as Italy, conventional individual company accounts show provisions for bad debts as a liability item rather than as a deduction from the asset debtors.

Foreign currency debtors in a company's balance sheet might be shown at either the transaction rate or the balance sheet rate. In the UK, Ireland and the Netherlands the balance sheet rate is used. The transaction rate would be regarded as irrelevant; and the balance sheet rate as the better guess for the future settlement rate.

In Germany and Sweden, foreign currency debtors are valued at the lower of the amounts that would be calculated under the transaction and balance sheet rates (see box below). This is a further example of conservatism. In France, company accounts and tax accounts use transaction rates, but group accounts may use the closing rate.

Foreign Currency Debtors (Germany, Henkel)

'Accounts receivable and payable in foreign currency are translated in the financial statements of individual companies at the rates of exchange in force when they first originated. If, however, translation of foreign currency items at the rate in force on the balance sheet date produces a lower or higher amount respectively, then foreign currency items are translated at the rates in force on the balance sheet date.'

6.5 Net Assets

Analysts will often be interested in arriving at a total of 'net assets', which is usually the same as 'shareholders' funds' (except that minority interests are not usually included in the latter but should probably be included in the former).

Clearly, all the points above in this chapter will affect these totals, but there are further problems relating to exactly which 'liabilities' to deduct in the calculation of net assets. This point was illustrated for France in section 2.4, where it was seen that some provisions are really reserves, meaning that they should not be included in shareholders' funds and not deducted in the calculation of net assets. (Provisions and reserves are discussed further in section 7.2.)

A German illustration was also begun by looking at the income statement effects (in Table 2.1). Table 6.1 overleaf shows the capital and liabilities side of a German consolidated balance sheet (the full balance sheet is shown on p 138). The very large figure for 'other accruals' (*sonstige Rückstellungen*)

*Table 6.1   Extract from Consolidated Balance Sheet of AEG Group as of
31 December 1988*

	Million DM	Million DM
Shareholders' Equity and Liabilities		
Equity		
Subscribed capital	931	
Capital reserves	885	
Revenue reserves	86	
Net profit of AEG AG	9	
Minority interests	78	
		1,989
Special Untaxed Reserves		**5**
Accruals		
Accruals for pensions and similar obligations	2,679	
Other accruals	1,851	
		4,530
Financial Liabilities		**598**
Other Liabilities		
Trade payables	1,068	
Payables to affiliated companies	582	
Other liabilities	604	
		2,254
		9,376

cannot be 'accruals' in the UK sense, for this would be some minor year-end adjustments such as unpaid wages or electricity bills. Such amounts would be shown as a last item in a German balance sheet (*Rechnungsabgrenzungsposten*). The expression 'other accruals' is a further example of inevitable pitfalls in translation.

The question here is how much of these provisions are like those 'provisions for contingencies' in section 2.4, ie how much are really reserves? The fact that the profit has been smoothed to zero suggests that 'other accruals' is at least partly the recipient of the double entries of the entries designed to achieve this. Unfortunately, it is impossible to disentangle the total; some of it is presumably 'contingencies' that would also be recognised in the UK.

The 'accruals for pensions' are not part of shareholders' funds. In a UK company, they would be separately held in a pension trust or in an independent company. A complication arises in that the pension fund may in some countries be over- or under-provided. If it is over-provided, part of it is really reserves. This is discussed and illustrated in section 7.4. Incidentally, if DM 2½ bn of the provisions are for pensioners, this implies that DM 2½ bn of the total assets (and the income on them) are for pensioners.

Starting from the top of the 'Equity' in Table 6.1, it is clear that the first four items are part of shareholders' funds. The implication of the order of items is that 'Minority interests' are also part of shareholders' funds. However, this results from the German 'entity view' that sees the parent shareholders and the minority shareholders as joint contributors to the capital. For analysts from most countries, minorities are excluded.

Next comes 'Special Untaxed Reserves'. These are amounts that have been charged against income in order to obtain a tax relief. They were not

Table 6.2   Extract from 'The Concise Key to Understanding Swedish Financial Statements' FAR, 1986

'Adjustments

Swedish financial statements can be basically adjusted to reflect US accounting principles as follows:

—Increase reported net income by 48% of the year's transfers to untaxed reserves; and

—Increase reported shareholders' equity by 48% of untaxed reserves in the balance sheet.

52% of each of these items represents deferred taxes.'

Table 6.3   Calculation of Shareholders' Funds for AEG Group

	DM m
Subscribed capital	931
Capital reserves	885
Revenue reserves	86
Net profit of AEG AG	9
Special untaxed reserves	5*
Other accruals	?

*or after deduction of corporation tax.

---

commercial expenses, so they are indeed 'reserves' in UK terminology. They should form part of shareholders' funds. There is one question, though: is it relevant that they would be taxable if they were to be returned back through the income statement in order to be distributed as dividends? If so, the tax rate on distributed income should be deducted (36% at the time of writing). As seen in Table 6.2 above, the Swedish accountancy body does think it relevant, but we could also ask: does the fact that a company cannot distribute share capital mean that the latter is not part of shareholders' funds? In other words: what is the relevance here of distributability or distribution?

An analyst is obviously in difficulty here, but Table 6.3 above summarises the discussion. Looking on the brighter side, since it is impossible to arrive at a useful profit number in this case (see Table 2.1), it does not matter that we cannot calculate shareholders' funds!

A further example of untaxed reserves may be useful. It is in Scandinavian countries that some of the greatest tax effects can be seen, so Sweden is taken as illustration here. Volvo, since it is registered with the SEC in the US, has to provide a reconciliation with US generally accepted accounting principles. Table 6.4 overleaf shows such a reconciliation, including the note on untaxed reserves.

Table 6.4   Extract from Volvo's Reconciliation to US GAAP

Net Income	**1986**	**1985**
Net income as reported in the Consolidated Statements of Income (in accordance with Swedish accounting principles)	2,551	2,546
Items increasing (decreasing) reported income:		
Allocations to untaxed reserves (Note A)	2,694	3,330
Income taxes	(1,547)	(1,975)
Tooling costs	110	323
Equity method investments	113	122
Write-down of investments	(500)	—
Business combinations	80	192
Foreign currency translation	(530)	(808)
Other	(15)	4
Net increase in income before extraordinary income	405	1,188
Income before extraordinary income	2,956	3,734
Extraordinary income	—	744
Approximate net income in accordance with US GAAP	2,956	4,478
Per share amounts, SEK:		
Income before extraordinary income	38.10	48.10
Extraordinary income	—	9.60
Approximate net income per share in accordance with US GAAP	38.10	57.70
Weighted average number of shares outstanding (in thousands)	77,605	77,605
Shareholders' equity		
Shareholders' equity as reported in the Consolidated Balance Sheets (in accordance with Swedish accounting principles)	10,124	8,798
Items increasing (decreasing) reported shareholders' equity:		
Untaxed reserves (Note A)	20,980	17,738
Income taxes	(11,950)	(10,279)
Tooling costs	1,269	1,159
Equity method investments	(233)	211
Business combinations	(282)	35
Other	184	142
Net increase in reported shareholders' equity	9,968	9,006
Approximate shareholders' equity in accordance with US GAAP	20,092	17,804

Note A. Allocations to untaxed reserves

Tax legislation in Sweden and certain other countries permits companies to make allocations to untaxed reserves, which are used principally to strengthen a company's financial position through the deferral of income taxes. To qualify as a tax deduction, Swedish tax law requires that these allocations must be deducted for financial reporting purposes. In accordance with US GAAP, such allocations are not recognized as a reduction of income for financial reporting purposes.

CHAPTER 7

Profit Measurement

Throughout Europe, the principles of prudence and accruals (matching) are used in profit measurement. These are specifically required by the EC's Fourth Directive, as is consistency of use of practices from year to year. Nevertheless, it is possible to give different emphases to these principles, and this is one reason why international differences in practice can result. In Chapter 6 the treatments of development expenditure and long-term contracts illustrate the conflict between accruals and prudence, and how it is resolved differently from country to country. This, and most other matters of valuation referred to earlier, affect profit measurement. A conservative valuation generally implies a conservative profit figure.

Several important areas of profit measurement are discussed below. As with valuation, most of the differences discussed in this chapter have so far survived EC harmonisation and will still be in place in 1992. Also, Appendices I and II contain reproduction of French and German company notes of relevance to this.

7.1 Depreciation

The basic divide in Europe is between those countries where depreciation in the financial statements is determined using accounting standards (the UK, Ireland and the Netherlands), and all other countries where tax rules play an important part. To take the example of the UK, there is a quite separate system of capital allowances, which are depreciation allowances for tax purposes. They are set by Parliament in order to achieve various economic aims, such as the encouragement of investment in depressed regions. This separation allows tax depreciation to achieve these aims and to be objective in size, whereas accounting depreciation can be determined by the use of judgment about scrap values, useful lives and nature of wearing out.

In the Netherlands, depreciation for tax purposes usually follows accounting depreciation, although it can be different. In cases of difference in these countries, it can be said that 'reversible timing differences' arise. That is, usually the main difference between tax depreciation and accounting depreciation is the *timing* of it not the eventual total of it. Tax depreciation often runs faster than accounting depreciation. Reversible timing differences lead to deferred tax, as discussed in the next section.

In most European countries, the tradition is that one of the main purposes of accounting has been for the collection of tax. Tax rules have dominated accounting rules. In Germany, the identity of tax and accounting rules is described as the *Massgeblichkeitsprinzip*. For example, in those cases where there are rapid tax depreciation allowances for regional development purposes, these uncommercially large charges must be recorded in the accounts in order to be allowable for tax purposes.

In many cases the tax rules allow depreciation charges that are broadly in line with what accountants would choose based on economic and physical factors. However, there will frequently be small differences and sometimes very large differences.

To some extent there has been a move away from this tax domination since the late 1980s in some countries. For example, in France it is possible to correct for these tax influences in group accounts. Throughout the EC, the Fourth and Seventh Directives require at least the disclosure of the effects of taxation rules. Where tax and accounting depreciation is the same, there can be no cause of deferred taxation.

In some countries, it is possible to revalue assets, as discussed in section 6.1. In such cases, depreciation charges would normally be raised in line with the revaluation of the assets. However, in France, where a general revaluation took place in 1978, depreciation charges are still reduced back to historical cost in order not to reduce taxable income. In French group accounts, this equalisation can be eliminated.

One peculiar feature of UK practice, as discussed in Chapter 5, is the annual revaluation of investment properties. This also has an effect on depreciation because the rules (SSAP 19) require that there shall not be systematic depreciation charges for investment properties. Further, a fairly common UK treatment of hotels, stores and similar properties is that they are not depreciated where it can be shown that repair and maintenance expenses are sufficient to keep the properties in at least as good a condition as when they were bought.

7.2   Deferred Tax

In the previous section, reversible timing differences between tax and accounting depreciation were shown to be a cause of deferred taxation. Other causes of reversible timing differences might be inventory valuation methods or instalment sales. In some countries, such as the USA, these differences are fully accounted for. That is, to continue with the example of accelerated tax depreciation, tax liabilities might be seen as artificially low in early years. Accounting for deferred tax corrects for this, as a result of the accruals convention.

The technique for achieving full accounting for deferred tax is to increase (*debit*) the tax for the year in the income statement to what it would have been without the generous tax rules. The counter-balancing effect is to create a deferred tax account (*credit*), which one could interpret as a liability to pay more tax in the future. Both accounting entries may seem unattractive to management: the debit makes earnings look lower; the credit makes liabilities look worse.

In the UK and Ireland, many reversible timing differences arise but standard practice is *not* to account fully for deferred tax. The method used is partial allocation, whereby deferred tax is only recognised as a liability when it is expected to be paid within the foreseeable future (normally three years). Some Dutch and Italian companies also follow this practice.

In most of continental Europe, deferred tax is not a major problem because of the close relationship between tax and accounting figures. However, in consolidated accounts, there may be foreign elements of deferred tax. Furthermore, in France, for example, consolidated accounts can now be freed from the dominance of tax; and, when values are changed from those in the individual company accounts, deferred tax may arise.

Throughout Europe, it is normal to use the 'liability' method, that is to take account of changes in the corporation tax rate because this will affect the amounts of future tax paid.

7.3 Provisions and Reserves

This matter has already been discussed in Chapter 2, but more detail is given here. An initial problem to address is that the words 'provision' and 'reserve' are used rather loosely. In English, this is the case in North America, where a provision for bad debts may be called an allowance or a reserve. For continental European accounts, after translation into American or British English, the subtleties of these words are frequently lost.

In the UK, a provision is an expense. It is, in a sense, an anticipation of a future expense or loss which is at present uncertain in size or probability. However, it usually relates to a past event: a bad debt provision relates to a past sale; a depreciation provision to past wearing out; a provision for a law suit to past unfair dismissals, etc. The provision leads to a charge to profit and to the setting up of a provision account, which is a liability account or a reduction in an asset account.

By contrast, a reserve is merely an allocation of the profit that has already been calculated. The reserve will often indicate that profits must not be depreciated (eg the legal reserve discussed in section 2.3) or that the directors intend not to distribute the profits.

Consequently, the distinction between provisions and reserves is of great importance. The setting up of a £1m provision has the effects of lowering earnings by £1m and raising liabilities (lowering net assets) by £1m. The setting up of a £1m reserve has no effect on any aggregates or ratios that analysts think important.

The difficulty for international analysis is that some continental companies make so-called provisions for no specific contingency: provisions for contingencies, provisions for general risks. French and German examples of these were given in section 2.4. There are also tax-based reserves, which are treated as provisions. In order to gain advantage of some tax law, a company must charge income with non-commercial tax 'expenses'. Some examples of this are shown in the box opposite.

> **TAX-BASED PROVISION**
> **(Germany, VEBA)**
>
> '(27) Other operating expenses
>
> These expenses include additions to reserves subject to future taxation of DM 14.4 million, compared to DM 4.4 million in the previous year.'
>
> **(Germany, Henkel)**
>
> 'The provision in the consolidated financial statements also includes corresponding amounts from the statements of other German companies, deferred tax liabilities of foreign companies, profits taxes on consolidation adjustments which will be subject to tax at later date, and the tax portion of special accounts and tax-allowable valuation adjustments still permitted under company law.'

Recently it has been possible in some countries to retain the advantage of tax-based provisions in company accounts, yet to move away from the accounting effects of this in consolidated accounts. In France, for example, although not all groups take advantage of this greater separation of tax from financial statements, it is normal for large listed companies. It is not normal for Germany.

7.4 Extraordinary Items

The definition of 'extraordinary' appears to be fixed in the Fourth Directive as 'otherwise than in the course of the company's ordinary activities'. However, in practice, the use of the term varies in Europe for several reasons:

(*i*)   The Directive is not in force in some countries: such as (at the time of writing) Spain, Italy, Portugal and, of course, Austria, Switzerland, Sweden, etc.

(*ii*) Some countries add glosses to the definition: eg in the UK and Ireland (SSAP 6), extraordinary items must also be material and not expected to recur.

(*iii*) Exactly what is 'ordinary activities' varies. For example, in the UK the sale of a shop by a stores group would not be thought to be extraordinary whereas it probably would be by a French stores group.

The example overleaf uses a public company in Denmark, where the Fourth Directive was implemented in 1981. Of the extraordinary expenses shown, only the second appears to fit the UK definition. Of the gains, the sale of tangible assets may well have been not extraordinary by UK standards.

EXTRAORDINARY ITEMS (Denmark, FLS Smidth & Co)

	KM
Note 5 Extraordinary income	
Profit on sale of site	144
Profits on sale of shares	50
Profits on sale of tangible assets	24
Other income	16
	234

Note 6 Extraordinary expenses	
Extraordinary losses on completed orders	44
Redundancy payments	35
Extraordinary write-offs on stocks and work in progress, etc.	31
Losses on sale of tangible assets	14
Losses on sale of properties	4
Other expenses	24
	152

(Note: the profit before extraordinaries was K 71M)

The important point is that 'earnings' as used in the UK *excludes* extraordinary items. Analysts may well wish to standardise on this but will be frustrated because of the differing definition. It may be necessary to standardise on profit after extraordinary items, because this is immune from the effects of the definition of extraordinary.

A further complication is the use in the UK and Ireland of the term 'exceptional items' (see Table 7.1 opposite). These are amounts which are *not* thought to be outside ordinary activities but are abnormal in size or incidence. In French, both extraordinary and exceptional are translated as 'exceptionnel', which hardly helps international analysis.

7.5 Pensions

The provision for pension costs can be a very large expense for many companies. It has become standard practice in the UK and the US to base a year's pension on an actuarial assessment of the degree to which the work done in that particular year will give rise to eventual pension payments. That is, the pay-as-you-go basis is not acceptable; under that system, a new company with a pension scheme but no pensioners would appear to have no pension costs.

However, even between the UK and the US, the differences of technical detail can lead to large differences in yearly charges. This is all the more so

Table 7.1   Consolidated Profit and Loss Account of Gallaher, 1987

Turnover	3,886.7
Cost of sales	(3.214.6)
Gross Profit	672.1
Distribution, advertising and selling costs	(392.1)
Administrative expenses	(101.6)
Other operating income	3.0
Trading profit before exceptional items	181.4
Exceptional items	—
Interest	(11.7)
Profit on ordinary activities before taxation	169.7
Tax on profit on ordinary activities	(62.5)
Profit on ordinary activities after taxation	107.2
Minority interests	(0.3)
Profit before extraordinary items	106.9
Extraordinary items	(5.5)
Profit for the financial year	101.4
Dividends paid	(44.4)
Profit retained for the year	57.0
STATEMENT OF RETAINED PROFITS	
At the beginning of the year	482.0
Profit retained for the year	57.0
Exchange adjustments on net investment in overseas subsidiaries	(6.1)
At the end of the year	532.0

for differences between the UK and continental Europe. If the rules for pension costs are lax, it becomes possible to charge too much or too little for pensions, and thereby to manipulate profits. For example, in Germany until 1987 year-ends, pension costs did not have to be charged. Consequently the Analysts Association (DVFA) always added back pension costs in order to get more comparable numbers within Germany.

Social conventions also affect this. The example in Table 7.2 overleaf uses UK, French and Italian companies. In all cases an amount has been charged, but the actual movement of funds may vary, which will certainly affect cash flow calculations based on income statements.

The British company places all pension provisions with a financial institution, and in this case, the 'funds' in question leave the company. For a company operating in France, there is a statutory requirement that part of the company's profits be allocated for the benefit of employees, with

Table 7.2   *Different Remuneration Methods and Funds*
Generated from Operations

	UK (£)	France (Francs)	Italy (Lire)
Earnings	100	1,000	100,000
Add back:			
Provision for employee pensions	80	—	—
less: funds applied in the current year	(80)	—	—
Share of profits attributable to employees	—	800	—
less: funds applied in the current year	—	(700)	—
Deferred employee remuneration	—	—	80,000
less: funds applied in the current year	—	—	(30,000)
Funds generated from operations*	100	1,100	150,000

*assuming no depreciation or other adjustments

Source: adapted from S J McLeay in C W Nobes and
          R H Parker, *Issues in Multinational Accounting*
          (Philip Allan, 1988).

reinvestment in external assets within two years. In the short term, there is an element in Funds Generated from Operations (+ F. 800 in the example) which is the accrual for the year, although only the cash outflow has actually been placed in external investments (− F. 700).

In Italy, employees are entitled on leaving a company to one month's salary (at current rates of pay) for each year in service. There is no requirement for the company to place these funds in earmarked investments, although the appropriate provisions must be made. Thus, Funds Generated from Operations includes the provision (+ L. 80,000) net of the cash payment to retiring employees (− L. 30,000).

7.6   The 'Bottom Line'

The section above has shown that it will usually be misleading to concentrate on any single line near the end of a profit and loss account. Apart from the problems of profit measurement and definition, there are also differences in presentation. The positioning of extraordinary items, taxes, dividends, minority interests and reserves varies.

(*i*)   *Extraordinaries*

In the UK and Ireland, extraordinaries are shown after 'profit on ordinary activities after taxation'. That is, tax is split between the amounts charged on ordinary and that on extraordinary profit. Table 7.1 shows an extract from a typical UK profit and loss account; the tax on extraordinary items could be shown on the face of the account but would normally be shown in a note.

By contrast, in most other countries, extraordinaries are shown gross of taxation and above the tax charge (see Table 7.3 below for Denmark, and Tables 7.4 overleaf or 2.1 for Germany).

In Germany, for example, there are several different types of taxes. So 'pre-tax' is ambiguous. (It should be noted that pre-tax profits in the UK are *after* some taxes, such as VAT and property rates.) Consequently, German companies do not always clearly show pre-tax profits (see Table 7.4).

(*ii*)   *Dividends*

In Tables 7.3 and 2.1, no dividends are shown as being paid. This is generally

Table 7.3   Profit and Loss Account of FLS Group, 1987 (Denmark)

	KM
Net sales (Note 1)	**7,166**
Cost of sales (Note 1)	(5,590)
Gross profit	1,576
Income from shares in subsidiaries (Note 2)	—
Interest receivable (Note 3)	823
Interest payable (Note 3)	
Sales and distribution costs (Note 1)	(622)
Administrative costs (Note 1)	(1,119)
Other operating income	58
Income from shares in associated companies (Note 4)	127
Income from other investments	21
Result before extraordinary items and tax	**71**
Extraordinary income (Note 5)	234
Extraordinary expenses (Note ?)	(152)
Provision for special contingencies	—
Result before tax	**153**
Tax on income for the year (Note 7)	(80)
Result after tax	**73**
Minority interests' share	(2)
Net result for the year	**71**

Table 7.4   Consolidated Statement of Income of the Henkel Group

| | 1987 | |
	DM'000	%
Sales	9,255,915	100.0
Cost of sales	5,409,579	58.4
Gross profit	3,846,336	41.6
Selling and distribution costs	2,378,617	25.7
Research and development costs	277,307	3.0
Administrative expenses	592,844	6.4
Other operating income	82,968	0.9
Other operating charges	106,455	1.2
Operating result	574,081	6.2
Financial items	− 42,934	−0.5
Result from ordinary activities	531,147	5.7
Extraordinary items	− 35,874	−0.4
Taxes on income	− 200,565	−2.2
Other taxes	− 2,708	—
Profit for the year	292,000	3.1
Allocation to revenue reserves	− 195,887	−2.1
Minority interests in profits	− 21,424	−0.2
Minority interests in losses	+ 1,611	—
Consolidated unappropriated profit	76,300	0.8

the case in continental Europe. In the UK and Ireland, a provision is made at the end of the year for the dividends proposed by the directors to be paid from the year's profits. This has to be approved by the AGM, but normally this is a formality. Therefore, the accruals convention suggests an accrual. In the accounts of a French company (though not necessarily of a group), there are two columns in a balance sheet, showing 'before allocation' (or 'before AGM decisions') and after (see Appendix I, p 133).

(iv)   Minority Interests

In some countries, for example Germany, the minority interests share of profit is not seen as a charge against earnings. This is because of the entity concept of the group or *Konzern*, that places less stress on the parent company shareholders. In Table 7.4, profit is shown before minorities. For most other countries, this is not the case: eg Denmark (Table 7.3) and the UK (Table 7.1). In the UK, minority share of profits is always extracted in the calculation of 'earnings'.

(v)   Reserves

In Table 7.4, the German company's reserve movements take place with items that would be included in earnings in the UK. In Table 2.1, another German company includes them in 'Group result'. By contrast, in the UK, reserve movements are clearly separated, or may be relegated to the notes. In France, the two-column approach (see (iii) above) handles the problem.

Of course, with two-sided accounts it is much more difficult to see what is going on. Two-sided accounts are still presented for individual companies in most European countries. The French example in the appendix to Chapter 5 illustrates this.

CHAPTER 8

Group Accounting

As discussed in section 2.6, consolidation is an invention that is only slowly spreading through Europe. By the end of the 1980s, it was still a rarity in many countries, even some in the EC. For example, one cannot yet rely on receiving consolidated accounts from Luxembourg, Spain or Switzerland.

So, it is particularly important to ascertain whether a set of accounts is consolidated or not. This is sometimes difficult; see Example 3 of section 5.3. In the absence of consolidated accounts, useful analysis without further information is impossible (see discussion surrounding Tables 2.3 and 2.4).

Given that a set of consolidated financial statements is available, it is then possible to grapple with the many areas where there are important international differences in treatment.

8.1   The Scope of 'The Group'

The purpose of consolidation is to present the accounts of the group as if it were a single entity. However, the exact scope of the group, and whether to consolidate all of it are debatable matters. The first question is whether the group is a set of enterprises under common control or those under common ownership? The logic of group accounting makes it clear that control is what really matters. Consequently, there is no debate that 100% of the assets, income, etc of a subsidiary should be consolidated even if it is only 75% owned. That amount of ownership will allow 100% control. This also makes it clear, for example, that a foreign subsidiary should be excluded from consolidation if the foreign government restricts management or bans distribution of profits. Doubts about control and about international accounting differences led German law to allow the exclusion of all foreign subsidiaries (until 1990 year-ends). However, most countries include normal foreign subsidiaries.

Where there is a sub-subsidiary in which the group owns 36%, this could easily still be controlled (see S_{11} in Table 8.1 opposite). Furthermore, in Table 8.1 the 45% holding in S_2 could make it a subsidiary if the remaining shares were widely spread and in practice exercised no control. French law imposes a rebuttable presumption that holdings of even 40% imply parentage. Traditional practice in the Netherlands and France has been to stress control as the criterion for consolidation.

Table 8.1 A Group Structure

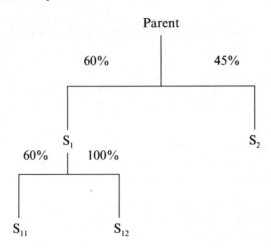

In the UK and Germany, by contrast, although control is seen as the reason for consolidation, ownership was seen as the most readily auditable proxy for the existence of control. Under the EC's Seventh Directive on company law (discussed in detail in Chapter 4) there are six identifiable criteria for consolidation, most of them rest upon ownership. Table 8.2 overleaf shows the UK definitions. Table 8.3 overleaf shows that there are international differences even within the EC and after the Seventh Directive. Despite these differences, in most cases a subsidiary is a company in which the group holds more than half the voting shares.

8.2 Associates and Joint Ventures

Some enterprises are not controlled by a group but are, nevertheless, significantly influenced by it. It has gradually become standard international practice to account for investments in such companies by a form of partial consolidation, usually called the equity method or one-line consolidation. Under this method, instead of bringing into the group balance sheet only the cost of the investment, the group's proportion of the equity (or net assets) of the enterprise is accounted for in a single line. In the UK and Ireland, such enterprises are called associates; in the US (and therefore by some continental countries) they are called, for example, 'companies consolidated by the equity method'.

In the group profit and loss account, the equity method involves taking the group's proportion of the net profit and tax of the associate. The normal position for this is 'above the line'; that is, included in earnings. This can be seen for the UK in Table 8.4 on p 93 (as 'related companies') and for

91

Table 8.2   Definitions of a Subsidiary (UK 1989 Act based on Seventh Directive)

Any one of the following will establish a parent/subsidiary relationship: where the parent,

1 (a) has the majority of voting rights; or
   (b) has the right to exercise dominant influence over the subsidiary because of a contract or provisions in the memorandum or articles; or

2 is a member of the subsidiary and
   (a) controls the majority of votes on the board of directors, or
   (b) controls by agreement the majority of voting rights; or

3 has a participating (20 + %) interest and
   (a) exercises dominant influence, or
   (b) manages on a unified basis.

Table 8.3   Implementation of Optional Elements of the Definition of a Subsidiary

	Art 1.1c* (parent as member)	Art 1.1c** (parent not member)	Art 1.2***
Belgium (draft)	Yes	Yes	No, but option
Denmark (draft)	Yes	No	No
France	Yes	No	No
Luxembourg	No	No	No
Netherlands	Yes	Yes	Yes
UK	Yes	Yes	Yes
West Germany	Yes	Yes (probably)	Yes

Notes   *   = an undertaking is a subsidiary if there is the right to exercise dominant influence over it by a shareholder in it.
    **   = as above, but the parent need not be a shareholder.
    *** = an undertaking is a subsidiary if there is exercise of dominant influence or unified management by another undertaking with a participating interest (eg, in the UK, a holding of 20% or more).

Denmark in Table 7.3. However, there can be variation. For example, some, but not all, French companies show income from associates near the end of the profit and loss account, as in Table 8.5 on p 94.

The exact definition of an associate can vary, but 'significant influence' is now generally presumed for investments of 20% to 50%. At one point in the Netherlands the threshold was 25% and in France $33\frac{1}{3}$%, but the Seventh Directive is harmonising on 20%. In some countries, the equity method was illegal (as in Germany until 1987 year-ends) or just not used. However, the Seventh Directive makes it compulsory (for example, in Germany from 1990 year-ends). In Sweden, most companies do not use the equity method because of doubts about its legality, despite a statement from the accountancy body (FAR) suggesting that it is acceptable in consolidated accounts. In the case of Volvo, the appropriate adjustment to US GAAP is shown in Table 6.4.

Table 8.4   Consolidated Profit and Loss Account of British Aerospace, 1988

	1988 £m
Turnover	5,639
Cost of sales	(5,328)
Trading Profit	311
Launching costs	(26)
Share of profits of related	17
Net interest payable	(66)
Profit Before Taxation and Exceptional Item	236
Exceptional item	—
Profit/(Loss) Before Taxation	236
Taxation	(80)
Profit/(Loss) After Taxation	156
Dividends	(53)
Balance Transferred To/(From) Reserves	103
Earnings/(Loss) Per Share	62.0p

Table 8.5   Consolidated Statement of Income of Bull, 1987

	FF'000s
Revenue:	
Sales	10,412,006
Rental, service and other	7,659,199
Total	**18,071,205**
Costs and Expenses:	
Cost of revenue	(10,545,231)
Research and development	(1,551,539)
Selling, general and administrative	(5,487,076)
Interest expense	(845,118)
Interest income	242,622
Other income—net	314,645
Total	**(17,871,697)**
Profit before Income Taxes, Extraordinary Credit and Minority Interests	**199,508**
Provision for income taxes	(1,021,317)
Extraordinary credit – income tax benefits of loss carryforwards	985,645
Minority interests	(8,629)
Share of the results of companies consolidated by the equity method	69,634
Net Income	**225,201**

Other non-EC countries are likely to follow the lead of the Seventh Directive. However, not all do so at present, as may be seen from the example below, where associates are not treated by the equity method:

ASSOCIATES (Switzerland, Adia)

'**Scope.** The consolidated statements include the figures of affiliated companies (which close their books at year end), according to the following criteria:

(*a*) For companies in the service sector:
When Adia SA owns over 50%, assets, liabilities, revenues and expenses are taken into account for 100%. The profit attributable to minority interests is deducted from the consolidated net profit under the heading "Minority Interests".

When Adia SA owns 50% or less, the consolidation takes into account the value of the investment and the dividends paid as booked in Adia SA.

(*b*) For all other Group companies:
Irrespective of the percentage held, only the value of the investment and the dividends paid are treated in the consolidation.'

In most countries joint ventures are treated as associates. However, the long-standing practice of some groups in France and the Netherlands is to use 'proportional consolidation' whereby the group's proportion of assets, liabilities, revenues and expenses are taken line-by-line into the group accounts. A typical note on this for a French company is reproduced below.

PROPORTIONAL CONSOLIDATION (France, Total Oil)

'Consolidation is, however, proportional, on the one hand for "joint interest" companies in which the holding is less than 50% and in which operations are shared on the basis of each partner's interest, and on the other hand for companies controlled jointly on a 50/50 basis by the Group and a single other shareholder.'

The Seventh Directive gives member states the option to allow proportional consolidation. This option has been taken, for example, in Germany, France and the Netherlands. However, in the UK the method is only available for unincorporated joint ventures.

8.3   Goodwill

Goodwill is the excess of the cost of an investment in a subsidiary (or associate or joint venture) over the proportion of net assets acquired. It is gradually becoming international practice for the net assets of the subsidiary to be measured at 'fair values' at the acquisition date for this purpose (as an estimate of 'cost' to the group). However, in most continental European countries, the traditional method has been to compare the cost of investment with the *book* value of the group's share of the subsidiary's net assets. This means a larger goodwill figure. The Seventh Directive requires the use of fair values or a method that gives similar results that is now used in Germany (see Table 5.5). Nevertheless, the book value method still continues in some EC and some other European countries.

Once goodwill has been calculated, at least three subsequent treatments can be found:

(i)   Leave the goodwill in the balance sheet at the acquisition level. This is not permissible under the Seventh Directive but is not unknown in Europe.

(ii) Show the goodwill as an asset but amortise it over its useful life. This is the predominant practice. French and Swedish companies often use 10 years; German companies 15 years.

(iii) Write the goodwill off immediately against reserves, thereby never showing an asset and never suffering amortisation charges. This is predominant practice in the UK and Ireland, and is common in the Netherlands.

8.4   Currency Translation

The Seventh Directive does not include rules relating to foreign currency translation. Consequently, the variety of practice in Europe is even greater for this topic than for other matters connected with consolidation. In the UK, Ireland and the Netherlands there is no law but there are 'standards' on the subject. However, in France and Germany there is no official guidance. In Sweden, the guidance from the accountancy body follows Anglo-American practice. In countries where there are no rules on consolidation, practice on translation is obviously varied.

Transactions

Discussion here will begin with the treatment of foreign currency items in an individual company's own accounts. In all countries it is normal to translate assets into local currency once and for all. For example, consider a British company that bought on credit a German computer invoiced in Deutsche-marks. In the UK accounts, and assuming no forward purchasing or matching, this asset would normally be frozen into pounds sterling at the date of purchase.

The next matter to consider is the resulting debtors or creditors in such cases. In most countries, if outstanding at a year-end, these amounts would be translated at year-end exchange rates. Thus, there would usually be gains or losses on settlement and at each year-end. However, some German, Swiss and Swedish companies take the conservative approach of recording debtors at the lower of the amounts in German currency at the date of sales and at the year-end. This was discussed in section 6.4.

Long-term liabilities in foreign currencies in an individual company's balance sheet are normally translated at year-end rates.

Losses recognised as a result of the above practices are generally taken immediately into the profit and loss account. However, the treatment of gains is more varied. In the UK gains on both short- and long-term monetary items are taken to profit, even though the gains are unsettled and unrealised. In the Netherlands, short-term gains are taken, but long-term gains are not always. In France, gains are not recognised for individual company accounts and for tax, but can be for consolidated accounts:

GAINS ON MONETARY ITEMS (France, Total Oil)

'Monetary assets and liabilities of the French companies denominated in foreign currencies are translated at the exhange rates ruling on 31 December. The resulting gains or losses are dealt with in the profit and loss account. Consequently the exchange difference accounts arising through the application of the French Revised Chart of Accounts are eliminated.'

In Germany, such gains are not recognised in individual or in group accounts.

Translation of Foreign Financial Statements

Companies in most countries use the current rate method for the translation of the accounts of foreign subsidiaries. This involves:

(*i*)   balance sheets translated at year-end rates,
(*ii*) profit and loss accounts translated at average rates for the year,
(*ii*) differences on translation put to reserves.

In the UK, SSAP 20 allows, and many companies use, the closing rate for profit and loss accounts.

In general, continental companies use the average rate for the profit and loss account (see, for example, Switzerland in Table 8.6 (p 98), France in Tables 8.7 and 8.8 (pp 99 and 100), and Germany in Table 8.9 (p 101). However, the treatment of exchange differences is not always uniform: note the treatment by Total Oil in Table 8.7 but the Anglo-American treatment by Bull in Table 8.8.

The major difference in Europe is in the differential use of the temporal method. This method, which used to be the standard US method in SFAS 8 from 1975 to 1981, requires the use of exchange rates that are appropriate to

(*text continues on p 102*)

Table 8.6   Swiss Currency Translation (Adia)

'The accounts of foreign Group companies are translated into Swiss francs according to the following rules: the profit and loss account items are translated by applying

— the annual average exchange rates (weighted in accordance with the monthly sales in the respective currencies) for sales and all other items of the profit and loss account, except the net profit figure;
— the actual exchange rates for the net profit of the year if already transferred;
— the average exchange rates for the month of December for the profit of the year if not yet transferred.

The differences arising from using the various exchange rates are grouped under the heading 'Non-operating income' in the consolidated profit and loss account. Balance sheet items are translated at the average exchange rates for the month of December.'

Table 8.7   French Currency Translation (Total Oil)

Foreign company balance sheets are converted into French francs on the basis of exchange rates at 31 December 1986. This conversion is applied to fixed assets as well as to monetary assets and liabilities. Gains or losses on translation of their balance sheets at the end of the previous year are dealt with:

— in reserves for that part which relates to non-monetary assets (property, plant and equipment, associated companies and trade investments).
— in the profit and loss account for that part which relates to monetary assets (long- and short-term debt and loans and cash balances) and stocks.

Average exchange rates are used for consolidated profit and loss account items so as to approximate to the figures that would be obtained by converting 1986 transactions on a daily basis. However, 'Net income' and 'allocations for depreciation and provisions' have been converted, in the same way as balance sheet items, using the rate at 31 December 1986.'

Table 8.8   French Currency Translation (Bull)

'The financial statements of the Group's foreign subsidiaries have been translated into French francs, for consolidation purposes, according to the principles of Statement No 52 of the Financial Accounting Standards Boards of the United States of America. These principles are summarized as follows:

- Assets and liabilities, including accumulated depreciation, are translated at year-end exchange rates.

- Income statement amounts are translated at average monthly rates of exchange.

Gains and losses resulting from translation are accumulated in a separate component of stockholders' equity entitled 'Translation adjustment'. The translation adjustments in 1987 and 1986 are reported on a separate line in the Consolidated Statement of Stockholders' Equity.'

Table 8.9   German Currency Translation (AEG)

'The fixed assets of consolidated foreign affiliates and the book values of the non-consolidated foreign affiliates are translated at the median currency exchange rate in effect at the year-end of the year of acquisition. All other assets, liabilities and equity are translated at the median exchange rate in effect at the end of the current year.

In the statement of income, revenue and expense items are translated at the average exchange rates of the current year. Exceptions are the depreciation of fixed assets and gains and losses on the disposal of fixed and financial assets, which are translated at the rates in effect at acquisition. Foreign affiliates' profits and losses for the year are translated at the median exchange rate in effect at the balance sheet date. The difference arising from translating at the average rate for the year and the rate in effect at year-end is included under other operating income or expenses.'

the valuation basis of the item to be translated. For example, fixed assets (and depreciation charges on them) and stocks held at historical cost are translated at the appropriate historical rates; most profit and loss account items can normally be translated at average rates; cash and debtors are translated at year-end rates.

In the UK SSAP 20 calls for the use of the temporal method for very closely held subsidiaries. In practice its use is very rare. SSAP 20 would call for differences on translation to be taken to the profit and loss account, as SFAS 8 used to require. The temporal method is rare in the Netherlands. In France, the closing rate and the temporal method are allowed, although the former is more common. The main exponents of the temporal method now are a number of German-based multinationals. They do not all take translation differences to reserves (see Table 8.9). Furthermore, the use of the temporal method is sometimes approximate; for example; some companies use the rates of the year-end of acquisition of an asset rather than the day of acquisition (again, see Table 8.9). Assuming that the Deutschemark is usually strong against currencies of subsidiaries, use of the temporal method will raise fixed asset values compared to use of closing rates of exchange, and depreciation charges will also be higher.

8.5 Segmental Reporting

The EC Directives require turnover to be split by sector and market. This latter requirement can be found in the laws that have implemented the Directives. In the UK, the practice of most large companies goes further because the Companies Act 1985 required pre-tax profit to be shown by sector. These requirements are also in the Listing Requirements of the International Stock Exchange in London. Further, in 1988 an Exposure Draft (No 45) was issued which would require disclosure of turnover, pre-tax profit and capital employed, by both sector and market. This approximates to US practice.

In general, practice in continental Europe does not go beyond that required by the rules implemented as a result of the Directive; and segmental reporting is not standard practice outside the EC.

CHAPTER 9

Conclusions

Financial reporting in Europe differs internationally for long-run, deep-seated reasons. However, as globalisation of the securities markets progresses and as the European community is moulded into a unified market, these accounting differences become obstructions. They make life more difficult for investors, lenders, traders, managers of companies, purchasers of companies, auditors, and so on.

Perhaps the greatest force for the removal of differences is commercial pressure. This probably explains the large number of annual reports from large continental European companies that are translated into English (often American English) and the widespread adoption of Anglo-American techniques such as the equity method of consolidation and lease capitalisation. However, this pressure operates selectively and without precision.

The EC Commission began to be an important force for accounting harmonisation in the late 1970s, with the effects being particularly noticeable by the late 1980s. Once the Seventh Directive has been implemented throughout the EC, a considerable degree of harmonisation will have been achieved compared to the situation in 1980. Nevertheless, many areas of practice are still very varied within the EC: fixed asset valuation, lease accounting, funds flow statements, currency translation. Eventually, more harmonisation will be achieved by commercial pressure and by EC Directives, but important differences will probably survive beyond the 1990s. This leaves investors, lenders, managers, auditors, analysts, etc with major problems of interpretation. These problems are compounded by language difficulties, upon which there are no current EC Directives but a considerable commercial pressure on some companies to use English.

In order to assist in the solution of these problems, this book has tried to lay bare the causes and nature of the international differences, and to analyse the harmonisation process. There is also a Glossary as Appendix III to help with some language difficulties. A further way of assistance is to summarise the main differences in the calculation of net assets and earnings. Most ratios depend on these latter two aggregates or figures that can be derived from them.

In Germany the Association of Investment Analysts (*Deutsche Vereinigung für Finanzanalyse und Anlageberatung*, DVFA) tries to adjust for the discretionary items in German accounts. Its objective is particularly to adjust earnings, not to a UK benchmark of course, but to a more comparable

103

German basis. The rules were rearranged in 1987 as a result of the implementation of the Fourth and Seventh Directives. Some of the main adjustments to German published net profit figures are:

(*i*) exclusion of all extraordinary and prior year items (even gains and losses on the sale of fixed assets which would be 'exceptional items' in the UK);
(*ii*) elimination of excess depreciation due to tax rules or for other reasons;
(*iii*) removal of the effects of changes to long-term provisions which are largely discretionary;
(*iv*) elimination of currency gains and losses on non-trading activities.

It is probable that most readers of this book will find a UK or US benchmark the most useful, not least because the numbers of listed companies is far greater in each of these two countries than in any continental European country. This chapter concentrates on a benchmark which is a version of UK practice. If a US benchmark is preferred, it will merely be necessary to be mindful of Anglo-American differences, as explained in the companion volume *Interpreting US Financial Statements*, Chapter 7.

Table 9.1   Some Main Areas of International Differences in Financial Reporting

1 Fairness
2 Taxation
3 Conservatism and Accruals
4 Provisions and Reserves
5 Valuation Bases
6 Consolidation
7 Uniformity and Accounting Plans
8 Shareholder Orientation of Financial Statements
9 Publication and Audit
10 Terminology
11 Formats

Let us start with a reminder of the differences examined in earlier chapters. Table 9.1 above contains the headings of Chapter 2 and some other major areas discussed elsewhere. A further reminder of differences is the classification of European countries shown in Table 3.3. All European countries except for the UK, Ireland and the Netherlands are shown there in the 'macro' group. For accounts from these countries, the following are some of the adjustments that may be necessary:

Action

1 Conservatism	INCREASE net asset values
2 Historical cost	INCREASE net asset values
3 LIFO	INCREASE inventory values for some
4 Translation	EXTRACT translation adjustments from German and other users of the 'temporal' method

5 Consolidation	BEWARE lack of consolidation
6 Associated Companies	INCREASE net assets and profit in cases of non-use of equity method
7 R and D	UK unusual in allowing capitalisation
8 Leases	INCREASE fixed assets and liabilities where leases are not capitalised
9 Pensions	EXAMINE carefully. EXTRACT any pension provisions from shareholders' funds.
10 Provisions	INCREASE shareholders' funds by portion of general provisions
11 Tax	DECREASE depreciation where caused by tax

In more detail, the benchmark towards which one might wish to work for international purposes could have the following features:

1   Earnings
(*i*)   after depreciation, interest, tax and preference dividend, minority profits,
(*ii*)   excluding extraordinary items,
(*iii*)   historical cost numbers,
(*iv*)   provisions for risks or contingencies not charged against profit,
(*v*)   tax-based provisions and depreciation not charged,
(*vi*)   all subsidiaries included,
(*vii*)   excluding differences on translation of foreign financial statements, but including exchange differences on transactions, loans, etc,
(*viii*)   excluding amortisation of goodwill,
(*ix*)   including share of profits of associated companies (20–50%),
(*x*)   excluding depreciation of set-up costs which should be charged in one year,
(*xi*)   interest expensed not capitalised,
(*xii*)   deferred tax not accounted for, except when expected to be paid soon.

2   Net Assets
(*i*)   standardise on historical cost for most assets but, if possible, current value of property,
(*ii*)   exclude capitalised goodwill, set-up costs, interest,
(*iii*)   deferred tax treated as reserve unless expected to be paid soon, when it is a provision,
(*iv*)   minorities included,
(*v*)   all subsidiaries included,
(*vi*)   closing rate translation,
(*vii*)   associates treated by equity method,
(*viii*)   tax-based provisions and those for risks or contingencies treated as reserves,
(*ix*)   leases capitalised.

Of these various adjustments, some will be simple from published accounts

105

and some will be capable of estimation. However, some problems will not be soluble from published information, although analysts may find that the above list raises useful questions to be asked at meetings with companies.

In summary, it is likely to remain impossible for many years to achieve precise comparisons of earnings or net assets figures across Europe. However, this does not mean that users of financial statements should just give up and pretend that all companies are using the same rules. Approximate adjustments and informed questions will lead to better decision-making.

Appendices

Extract from the Annual Report of Total Oil, 1988

TOTAL GROUP
CONSOLIDATED ━━━━━━━
FINANCIAL STATEMENTS

AUDITORS' REPORT

Ladies and Gentlemen,

In accordance with our appointment at the Annual General Meeting on 20 June 1986, we present our report on :

- the audit of the consolidated accounts of TOTAL Compagnie Française des Pétroles which are attached to this report,

- the verifications of the management report,

relating to the year ended 31 December 1988.

OPINION ON THE CONSOLIDATED ACCOUNTS

We have audited the consolidated accounts by carrying out such procedures as we considered necessary in accordance with standards of the profession.

The basis of consolidation has been amended in accordance with new French regulations. The accounts for 1987 have been restated to incorporate these changes. Details of these adjustments and their effect on the 1987 accounts are set out in note 3.

We certify that the consolidated accounts comply with the legal requirements and give a true and fair view of the assets, the financial position and the results of the companies included in the consolidation.

SPECIFIC VERIFICATION

We are satisfied that the information included in the management report is fairly presented and is consistent with the consolidated accounts.

Paris, 27 April 1989

The Auditors
Members of Compagnie de Paris

CABINET CAUVIN, ANGLEYS, SAINT-PIERRE, REVIFRANCE

FRINAULT-FIDUCIAIRE

F. ANGLEYS   R. AMIRKHANIAN

G. BARTHES de RUYTER   M. LEGER

CHARTERED ACCOUNTANTS' REPORT
TO THE CONSEIL D'ADMINISTRATION

Gentlemen,

In connection with the listing of the Company's shares on the Stock Exchange in London, we have reviewed the audited accounts of the TOTAL Group and of the parent company TOTAL Compagnie Française des Pétroles (TOTAL CFP) for the year ended 31 December 1988.

The accounting requirements of the Seventh Directive of the EEC have been applied to the consolidated accounts for the year under review. We note that Group accounting policies have been changed to follow the principles of the International Accounting Standards Committee. We set out below our comments on significant variations which would arise if the accounts had been prepared in accordance with United Kingdom accounting requirements.

- The emphasis would be on the Group accounts, and there would not be separate presentations for the holding Company and for the Group. In particular detailed information on the profit and loss account of the holding company would not be required.

- The consolidated balance sheet would show the state of affairs of the Group on the basis that the proposed dividends and other appropriations recommended by the directors would be approved and it would therefore be shown after allocation of profits. Similarly, the holding company's accounts would take credit for dividends proposed but not yet paid by the subsidiaries out of their profits.

- Extraordinary and exceptional items would be dealt with separately. Exceptional items would be included in the profit on ordinary activities before taxation and disclosed in the notes. Extraordinary items (less attributable taxation) would be shown separately in the profit and loss account after the results derived from ordinary activities after taxation.

- Joint interest and jointly controlled companies would be treated as associated companies. They would be consolidated using the equity method, and not the proportional method, which treats such companies as if they were unincorporated joint ventures. Where the Group's interest in joint interest and jointly controlled companies is greater than 50 % the method of consolidation in the UK would be full consolidation.

- For associated companies, the notes would disclose the Group's share of profits before tax, tax charge, extraordinary items and accumulated net profits retained together with loans to and from such companies.

- The notes would include totals of authorized capital commitments distinguishing between those contracted for and those not contracted for.

- Financial costs included in the capital cost of fixed assets would be disclosed both for the amounts capitalized in the year and for amounts carried in the balance sheet at the end of the year.

- The provisions of the Statement of Recommended Practice issued by the Oil Industry Accounting Committee would be followed. In particular, supplementary financial information would be provided on capitalized exploration, production and pre-production costs, decommissioning costs, and further analysis of the results of oil and gas operations.

London, 27 April 1989

STOY HAYWARD
Chartered Accountants

CONSOLIDATED BALANCE SHEET AT 31 DECEMBER 1988
(F. million)

ASSETS

	31/12/1988	31/12/1987 restated	31/12/1987 before restatement
FIXED ASSETS	44 833	36 385	34 651
Intangible assets (note 4)			
. Gross amount	2 645	1 369	1 420
. Less depreciation and provisions	- 572	- 402	- 526
	2 073	967	894
Tangible assets (note 5)			
. Gross amount	65 239	54 685	72 224
. Less depreciation and provisions	- 32 374	- 28 144	- 46 053
	32 865	26 541	26 171
Financial assets			
. Investments in associated companies	1 118	1 267	1 252
. Other fixed asset investments (note 6)	3 961	3 241	3 231
. Other financial assets (note 7)	4 816	4 369	3 103
	9 895	8 877	7 586
CURRENT FINANCIAL ASSETS	673	950	950
CURRENT ASSETS	42 441	37 699	36 909
Inventories (note 8)	8 593	8 528	8 626
Trade and related debtors	12 005	10 357	10 409
Other debtors	5 093	4 137	4 298
Listed investments	4 125	3 385	3 385
Liquid assets and short term deposits	12 625	11 292	10 191
TOTAL	87 947	75 034	72 510

LIABILITIES

	before income allocation		
	31/12/1988	31/12/1987 restated	31/12/1987 before restatement
CAPITAL AND RESERVES	23 293	21 617	23 289
Issued share capital	1 816	1 812	1 812
Share premium account	2 971	2 959	2 959
Consolidated reserves	16 348	15 923	17 062
Exchange differences	679	- 393	-
Shareholders' funds (note 10)	21 814	20 301	21 833
TOTAL CFP share of consolidated results	1 479	1 316	1 456
NON-VOTING PREFERENCE SHARES ISSUED BY CONSOLIDATED SUBSIDIARIES (note 9)	1 620	534	-
MINORITY INTERESTS (note 10)	3 631	2 717	3 211
GRANTS	-	-	387
PROVISIONS FOR RISKS AND CHARGES	11 500	11 507	8 053
Provisions for deferred taxes (note 11)	4 541	4 112	3 170
Provisions for pensions and similar commitments (note 12)	3 955	4 123	2 058
Other provisions for risks and charges (note 13)	3 004	3 272	2 825
LONG TERM LIABILITIES	15 604	12 901	12 871
Loans and finance creditors (note 14)	15 015	12 346	12 316
Deposits received as security repayable after more than one year	589	555	555
SHORT TERM LIABILITIES	32 299	25 758	24 699
Loans and finance creditors	13 692	8 802	7 662
Trade and similar creditors	9 474	7 960	7 676
Other creditors	9 133	8 996	9 361
TOTAL	87 947	75 034	72 510

CONSOLIDATED PROFIT AND LOSS ACCOUNT
(F. million)

	Year 1988	Year 1987 restated	Year 1987 before restatement
Turnover (note 15)	83 290	86 743	87 087
Operating expenses (note 16)	- 71 598	- 76 601	- 75 901
Depreciation (note 17)	- 4 824	- 3 679	- 4 582
OPERATING INCOME	6 868	6 463	6 604
Financial income (note 18)	1 835	1 696	1 696
Financial charges	- 2 508	- 1 914	- 1 852
OPERATING PROFIT BEFORE TAXATION	6 195	6 245	6 448
Taxes (note 19)	- 5 293	- 6 328	- 6 277
Other expenses and income (note 20)	974	1 224	1 254
Share of profits of associated companies	79	134	125
GROUP'S NET CONSOLIDATED RESULT	1 955	1 275	1 550
Minority interest	476	- 41	94
TOTAL CFP NET CONSOLIDATED RESULT	1 479	1 316	1 456
CONSOLIDATED EARNINGS PER SHARE (in francs) calculated on the basis of the number of shares in issue at 31 December	41	36	40

STATEMENT OF SOURCE AND APPLICATION OF FUNDS
(F. million)

	Year 1988	Year 1987 restated
SOURCE OF FUNDS		
Funds generated from operations :		
- Group's net consolidated result	1 955	1 275
- Depreciation	4 824	3 679
- Long-term provisions	- 765	615
- Exploration costs written off	1 139	859
Total funds generated from operations	7 153	6 428
Investment disposals at net book value	2 250	2 630
Increases in capital	336	172
Issue of non-voting preference shares	909	534
Movement in long and medium-term debt	1 977	- 704
TOTAL SOURCES	12 625	9 060
APPLICATION OF FUNDS		
Capital investments - gross	14 352	8 546
Purchases of shares from minorities	583	411
Dividends paid	850	882
Other	- 314	694
	15 471	10 533
Working capital movement	- 2 846	- 1 473
TOTAL APPLICATION	12 625	9 060
WORKING CAPITAL MOVEMENT		
Stocks	- 86	- 322
Other current items	- 2 760	- 1 151
TOTAL	- 2 846	- 1 473

115

NOTES

1. ACCOUNTING POLICIES

The Group's consolidated accounts have been prepared in accordance with the French law of 3 January 1985 and the statutory instrument of 17 February 1986.

They are in accordance with the accounting principles issued by the International Accounting Standards Committee (IASC). As an exception, in accordance with French law, the accounts of jointly-controlled subsidiaries are consolidated on a proportional basis.

BASIS AND METHOD OF CONSOLIDATION

Companies eligible for consolidation are those over which TOTAL Compagnie Française des Pétroles control is at least 20 %. The parent company's share of the equity of such companies or the TOTAL Group's investment therein (investments and long-term loans) must in addition represent at least F 20 million.

The minimum value criterion is not applied to certain companies due to the importance of their operations to the Group, nor to sub-participations whose accounts are already included in a consolidated sub-group.

Full consolidation is applied in the case of companies which are more than 50 % controlled by the Group. Exceptions to this rule may be made in the case of subsidiaries which are less than 50 % controlled but over the management of which the Group has the main influence.

Consolidation is proportional for companies controlled jointly with other shareholders or partners.

All the other companies have been accounted for on an equity basis. The Group's share of these companies' earnings is included in the consolidated statement of income.

CURRENCY TRANSLATION

Monetary transactions

Monetary assets and liabilities in the balance sheets of the consolidated companies which are denominated in foreign currencies are translated at the exchange rates ruling on 31 December. The resulting losses or gains are dealt with in "Other expenses and income" in the statement of income. However, where foreign currency loans are contracted in order to protect a net investment in a foreign company from the effect of exchange rate fluctuations, differences on exchange from these loans and investments are offset.

Translation of financial statements denominated in foreign currencies

The balance sheets of foreign subsidiaries are converted into French francs on the basis of exchange rates at 31 December. Translation differences are dealt with as follows :

- for the Group share, as a movement on reserves in "Exchange differences",

- for the minority share, in "minority interest."

Profit and loss account items are converted as follows :

- Results, depreciation, and provisions : at the exchange rate ruling on 31 December.

- Other items : at the average rate for the year. Differences on exchange between the rate ruling at 31 December and the average rates are dealt with in "Exchange differences" in the profit and loss account.

EXPLORATION/PRODUCTION COSTS

The Group uses the "successful efforts" method of accounting for exploration and production costs, defined in standard 19 of the Financial Accounting Standards Board (FASB), as follows :

Mineral rights :

These are capitalized and provisions made against their cost in the absence of a commercial discovery.

Exploration costs :

- geological and geophysical survey expenses are charged directly against income.

- expenditure on wells where commercially exploitable reserves have not been discovered are charged directly against income.

- expenditure on wells in progress and wells where proven reserves have been discovered are capitalized.

Capitalized production costs :

- Development costs are capitalized.

- Finance costs attributable to the development of proved reserves are capitalized as a cost of development until production commences.

Depreciation of exploration and production assets :

All assets related to production (mineral rights, exploration and production wells and related facilities) are depreciated by the unit-of-production method.

The annual charge is obtained by multiplying the net value of the asset by the following factor :

$$\frac{\text{Production for the year}}{\text{Proven reserves at end of year + production for the year}}$$

Limitation of net value of capitalized costs :

When the net value of oil and gas assets country by country at the end of the year exceeds the corresponding future net revenues, a provision for depreciation of the assets is made.

Treatment of production sharing agreements :

These agreements are signed by oil companies with host states for their exploration and production activities. The host state is represented by a publically owned National Company, to which the State grants all mineral rights and, consequently, the ownership of any future production arising from such rights.

The oil company finances all the exploration and development carried out on behalf of the State company. In the event of production, the oil company receives a contractual proportion of such production to reimburse its advances and produce a profit.

Where commercially viable reserves are not discovered, exploration costs are not reimbursed to the oil company.

Exploration and production expenses incurred under these contracts are carried under "Other financial assets". They are evaluated and provided against according to the successful efforts method.

INTANGIBLE ASSETS

Goodwill is amortized in the consolidated profit and loss account over a period not exceeding 10 years.

TANGIBLE ASSETS

These are included in the consolidated balance sheet at their purchase price. Fixed assets acquired by French companies before 1976 are included at the amounts derived from the legal revaluation at that time as stated in their own accounts, and revaluations by foreign sub-sidiaries (excluded from their own accounts) are treated similarly. Assets are depreciated on the straight-line basis over their useful lives.

Fixed assets of significant value which are held under finance lease agreements are capitalized and amortized on the straight-line basis. The corresponding obligation is included as a liability.

Investment grants are deducted directly from the cost attributed to the fixed asset.

OTHER FIXED ASSET INVESTMENTS

These are accounted for at their cost of acquisition, and where appropriate, provisions are made according to the underlying net assets, economic value and percentage shareholding.

Dividends received from non-consolidated subsidiaries are dealt with in financial income when received.

INVENTORIES

Stocks of crude oil and refined products are valued at cost on the FIFO basis ; the value of other stocks is generally calculated at the lower of cost or net realizable value.

RESEARCH AND DEVELOPMENT EXPENSES

These are charged to the year in which they are incurred.

PENSIONS AND SIMILAR COMMITMENTS

In accordance with the laws and practices of each country, the Group makes provision for retirement pensions for its employees, generally through contributions to the bodies responsible for payment of these retirement benefits.

The commitments made by the Group are accounted for on an actuarial basis of rights acquired by the beneficiaries and recorded in "provisions for pensions and similar commitments" as liabilities. They correspond to retirement benefit rights acquired by current and retired employees and to payments for early retirement.

TAXATION

Current taxation

Current taxation comprises actual tax charges, including

NOTES

taxes payable to producing countries, and withholding taxes payable by way of decisions by consolidated subsidiaries to make distributions.

Under the agreement for taxation of worldwide profits which applies to the consolidated profits of TOTAL CFP, amounts repayable for the current year in respect of consolidated subsidiaries have been set off against taxation in the profit and loss account.

Deferred taxation

Deferred taxation is provided under the liability method, in order to take into account :

. timing differences in tax charges which arise as a result of variations between taxable profit and the pre-tax profits of subsidiaries.

. restatements in company accounts on consolidation.

Deferred tax net debit balances are not treated as assets.

Under the agreement for taxation of worldwide profits applicable to TOTAL CFP, taxation payable by French subsidiaries is offset against deferred taxation equivalent to the deferred repayment due. This taxation is eliminated on consolidation in proportion to the Group's interest in the tax paid, up to a maximum of the tax credits repayable.

TURNOVER

Turnover is stated net of duties and sales taxes.

STATEMENT OF SOURCE AND APPLICATION OF FUNDS

The statement of source and application of funds is drawn up from actual operations for the year and not by a mere comparison of balance sheets. The effects of variations in consolidation methods and fluctuations in exchange rates are therefore eliminated.

Acquisitions and disposals of consolidated subsidiaries are shown by substituting the values of the underlying assets and liabilities in place of the investment.

Funds generated from operations is stated before deducting depreciation, long term provisions and costs of exploration investments which have not resulted in discoveries of commercially viable reserves. It includes the Group's share of the results of subsidiaries consolidated under the equity method together with profits and losses on disposals of assets.

Disposals of investments are shown at net book value.

2. CONSOLIDATED COMPANIES

SEE TABLE OPPOSITE

3. MODIFICATION OF CONSOLIDATION PROCEDURE – CHANGES IN THE COMPOSITION OF THE GROUP

MODIFICATION OF CONSOLIDATION PROCEDURE

The decree of 17 February 1986 relating to consolidated accounts permitted the use of methods previously applied, subject to some restrictions, until the 1987 accounts. The TOTAL Group took advantage of this provision but has modified the methods used to prepare its 1988 accounts in order to conform with the new regulation.

For the application of the new French regulations concerning consolidated accounts, the Commission des Opérations de Bourse and the Conseil National de la Comptabilité recommend that the effects of the changes in consolidation procedure be applied to shareholders' funds. The TOTAL Group has followed this recommendation and restated the 1987 consolidated accounts to permit comparison with 1988.

PRINCIPAL CHANGES IN CONSOLIDATION PROCEDURE - EFFECT ON THE 1987 ACCOUNTS (MF)

The effect of the changes in accounting policies on the balance sheet at 31 December 1987 is a reduction in shareholders' funds of 1 531, and a reduction in the Group share of the consolidated profits of 140.

The principal changes in accounting policies are as follows :

- The balance sheets of foreign subsidiaries are converted into French francs at the rate ruling at 31 December. Exchange differences on monetary items, which used to be included in the result for the year, have been restated as a movement on reserves.

Effect on the 1987 accounts :

```
. Group shareholders' funds ................ -    89
. Group share of results ................... +    89
```

2. CONSOLIDATED COMPANIES

For the year 1988, the Group is made up of 218 companies of which 195 are fully consolidated, 3 are consolidated on a proportional basis and 20 are accounted for under the equity method.

PRINCIPAL SUBSIDIARIES AND RELATED COMPANIES

EXPLORATION - OIL PRODUCTION

		Group's interest
	TOTAL Exploration /France	100.0
	TOTAL Oil Marine /Great Britain	100.0
	TOTAL Marine Norsk /Norway	100.0
	TOTAL Marine Exploitatie /Netherlands	100.0
	TOTAL Mineraria /Italy	99.9
	TOTAL Energia Italiana Spa	99.8
	Compagnie Française des Pétroles (Algérie)	100.0
	TOTAL Algérie	100.0
	TOTAL Proche-Orient /Egypt	99.6
E	Abu Dhabi Petroleum Company	23.8
E	Abu Dhabi Marine Areas	33.3
	TOTAL Abu Al Bu Khoosh /Abu Dhabi	99.6
E	Dubai Marine Areas	50.0
	TOTAL Aden Exploration Production /S.Yemen	99.8
	TOTAL Syrie	99.8
	TEPCAM /Cameroon	79.0
	TOTAL Angola	100.0
	TOTAL Exploratie en Produktie /Kenya - Colombia - N. Yemen	100.0
	TOTAL Indonésie	100.0
	TOTAL Chine	99.6
	TOTAL Austral /Argentina	99.8
	Consolidated Trans-Canada Resources Ltd	45.1
	Ranchmen's Resources Ltd /Canada	37.9

TRANSPORT

		Group's interest
	TOTAL Compagnie Française de Navigation	99.5
E	Pipeline Méditerranée Rhône	30.8
	TOTAL Transport Ltd /International	99.9
	TOTAL Transport Corporation /International	100.0

REFINING - MARKETING

		Group's interest
	Compagnie de Raffinage et de Distribution	
	TOTAL FRANCE	96.2
	Totalgaz (CFGL)	96.2
	Stela	96.1
	Les Fils Charvet	91.6
	Docks des Alcools	56.2
	Société Anonyme des Pétroles Mory	100.0
	Air TOTAL France	100.0
	Air TOTAL Suisse	99.9
	Air TOTAL International	99.0
	TOTAL Oil (Great Britain) Ltd	100.0
P	Lindsey Oil Refinery /Great Britain	50.0
	TOTAL Belgique	100.0
	TOTAL Nederland	100.0
P	TOTAL Raffinaderij Nederland	55.0
	Deutsche TOTAL	100.0

REFINING - MARKETING (CONT'D)

		Group's interest
	Defrol /Germany	100.0
	TOTAL Espana	100.0
	TOTAL Hellas /Greece	100.0
E	TOTAL Maroc	50.0
	TOTAL Afrique	100.0
	TOTAL Sénégal	78.6
	TOTAL Côte d'Ivoire	75.8
	TOTAL Nigeria	60.0
	TOTAL Cameroun	65.0
	TOTAL Fina Gabon	54.0
	TOTAL Oil Products - East Africa	78.6
	TOTAL South Africa Pty	57.6
	TOTAL Réunion Comores	100.0
	TOTAL Pacifique	100.0
E	Raffinerie des Antilles	25.0

CHEMICALS - FERTILIZERS

		Group's interest
	TOTAL Chimie	100.0
E	Socabu	20.0
	Pétroplastique SNC	96.2
	Hydrocarbures de Saint-Denis	84.5
	Hutchinson (pre-consolidated)	80.8
E	Ruwais Fertilizer Industries Ltd /Abu Dhabi	33.3

COAL - MINERALS - SOLAR ENERGY

		Group's interest
	TOTAL Compagnie Minière	100.0
	TOTAL Compagnie Minière France	100.0
	TOTAL Energie Développement	96.6
	TOTAL Exploration South Africa	85.1
	TOTAL Energold Corporation /Canada	71.1
	Minatco Ltd /Canada	100.0
	TOTAL Mining Australia Pty Ltd	100.0
E	Golconda /Australia	24.8

FINANCE - OTHER - MULTIPLE ACTIVITIES

		Group's interest
	TOTAL Compagnie Française des Pétroles	100.0
	TOTAL International Ltd /International	100.0
E	Compagnie Générale de Géophysique	23.9
	OFP - Omnium Financier de Paris	52.5
	Société Financière d'Auteuil	51.5
	Omnium de Pétroles S.A. (OPSA)	52.5
	Omnium Insurance and Reinsurance Co.	88.0
	TOTAL Petroleum (North America)	50.9
	TOTAL Energy Resources Inc. /United States	100.0
	TOTAL Resources Canada Ltd	100.0
	TOTAL Australia Ltd	100.0

P = Consolidated companies whose accounts are prorated according to the Group's ownership

E = Equity method of accounting

Geographical base of subsidiaries : shown with a stroke after the company's name where necessary.

N.B. : In the case of consolidated companies the percentage of interest represents the Group's share in their shareholders' funds and result. This percentage may be different from the controlling interest in the case of sub-participations.

NOTES

- The accounts of oil exploration/production subsidiaries have been restated according to the successful efforts method.

Effect on the 1987 accounts :

. Group shareholders' funds .... -	154
. Group result .... -	34
. Value of net fixed assets .... + 1	247
. Provisions for deferred taxation .... + 1	025
. Provisions for risks .... +	362

- Significant lease contracts have been capitalized.

Effect on the 1987 accounts :

. Group's shareholders' funds .... -	12
. Group result .... -	44
. Minority interest .... -	8
. Value of net fixed assets .... + 1	123
. Value of long term debts .... + 1	080

- Provisions for pensions and similar commitments which are included in contingent liabilities have been provided for as long term liabilities.

Effect on the 1987 accounts :

. Group shareholders' funds .... - 1	429
. Group result .... -	62
. Minority interest .... -	574
. Provisions for pensions and similar commitments .... + 2	065

- Non-voting preference shares issued by consolidated North American subsidiaries, which are redeemable at the option of the issuing companies, used to be included in long term liabilities, and have been restated and included in the account "Non-voting preference shares issued by consolidated subsidiaries.

Effect on the 1987 accounts :

. Non-voting preference shares .... +	534
. Long term liabilities .... -	534

CHANGES IN GROUP STRUCTURE

TOTAL Resources Canada, a 100 % subsidiary of TOTAL CFP acquired Getty Resources Ltd, which has changed its name to TOTAL Energold Corporation, for a consideration of 721 MF.

During the first quarter of 1988, TOTAL Compagnie Française des Pétroles made a public offer to purchase shares in CRD TOTAL FRANCE. Following this offer, the Group has increased its percentage interest in CRD TOTAL FRANCE from 30.31 % to 96.2 %.

The overall cost of acquisition amounted to 867 MF.

---

4. INTANGIBLE ASSETS

(MF)

	31 December 1988		31 December 1987 - Restated -	
	GROSS	DEPRECIATION	GROSS	DEPRECIATION
Deferred charges	72	58	181	136
Goodwill on consolidation	1 799	262	616	123
Other intangible assets	774	252	572	143
TOTAL	2 645	572	1 369	402

The change in "goodwill on consolidation" arises mainly from the cost of acquisition of the minority shares in CRD TOTAL FRANCE in the first quarter of 1988, for 867 MF.

5. TANGIBLE ASSETS

(MF)

ANALYSIS BY CLASS	31 December 1988		31 December 1987 - Restated -	
	GROSS	DEPRECIATION	GROSS	DEPRECIATION
Land	2 241	-	2 010	-
Production drilling	5 417	2 367	4 263	1 855
Processing plants and buildings	48 456	28 583	43 624	25 098
Oil exploration	6 747	1 353	2 802	1 151
Mining exploration	605	71	70	34
Assets under construction	1 773	-	1 916	6
TOTAL	65 239	32 374	54 685	28 144
Processing plants and buildings held under finance leases included above	2 154	831	1 735	612

Oil exploration costs directly charged to expenses and not incurred under production sharing agreements represent 841 MF in 1988 against 815 in 1987.

(MF)

ANALYSIS BY SECTOR OF OPERATION AT 31/12/88	Land and assets under construction	Other property, plant + equipment				Total	
		Gross value	Deprec- iation	Net value	Deprec- iation %	Gross value	Net value
	1	2	3	4	5	1 + 2	1 + 4
Exploration/Production	1 161	27 260	10 822	16 438	39	28 421	17 599
Transport/Refining/Marketing ...	2 332	27 302	18 417	8 885	67	29 634	11 217
Chemicals	143	2 911	1 657	1 254	57	3 054	1 397
Coal/Minerals/Solar energy	98	2 145	1 030	1 115	48	2 243	1 213
Other	280	1 607	448	1 159	37	1 887	1 439
TOTAL	4 014	61 225	32 374	28 851	53	65 239	32 865

121

NOTES

6. OTHER FIXED ASSET INVESTMENTS

This note provides details of the principal fixed asset investments which have not been consolidated :

(MF)

	% control at 31/12/88	Net book value of shares held by the Group at 31/12/88	100 % capital and reserves at 31/12/88 before results for 1988	100 % of 1988 result
Paribas	2.77	682	19 600	2 647
Abu Dhabi Gas Industries Ltd (GASCO) .	15.00	273	2 557	-
SAGA Petroleum	5.00	221	1 591	47
Lambert Frères	24.14	156	517	112
Marceau Investissement	6.67	120	1 815	40
Technip	13.33	112	334	60
Prétabail	13.59	112	1 194	236

7. OTHER LONG-TERM FINANCIAL ASSETS

(MF)

	31 December 1988		31 December 1987 - Restated -	
	GROSS	DEPRECIATION	GROSS	DEPRECIATION
Advances under production sharing contracts (oil and gas activity)				
. Exploration work without proven reserves ...	800	768	671	671
. Exploration and development of proven reserves	2 516	1 199	1 971	1 139
Other loans	4 543	1 076	4 656	1 119
TOTAL	7 859	3 043	7 298	2 929

8. INVENTORIES AND STOCK HOLDING MOVEMENTS

INVENTORIES

ANALYSIS BY CLASS OF STOCK	31 December 1988		31 December 1987 - Restated -	
	Thousand tonnes	Million F	Thousand tonnes	Million F
Crude liquid hydrocarbons	3 152	2 055	2 930	2 054
Petroleum products	5 174	4 854	4 930	5 188
Coal, uranium and other minerals		229		123
Other		1 455		1 163
TOTAL		8 593		8 528

STOCK HOLDING MOVEMENTS

The stock holding effect on the consolidated results is estimated each year by reference to the replacement cost of sales.

In 1988, the stock holding effect on the consolidated group was a negative 600 MF (of which 580 MF related to TOTAL CFP). In 1987, this effect was a positive 220 MF on the consolidated group (of which 120 MF related to TOTAL CFP).

9. NON-VOTING PREFERENCE SHARES ISSUED BY CONSOLIDATED SUBSIDIARIES

These shares are issued by North American consolidated subsidiaries and carry a dividend which, in the case of TOTAL Energy Resources Inc., depends upon the rate applicable to class AA commercial paper, and in the case of Ranchmen's, is at a fixed rate.

Dividends paid are included under the heading "Other income and expenses" in the profit and loss account.

	Millions of Foreign currency	Millions of French francs
Balance at 31 December 1987 (restated)	100 M$ US	534
Movements during 1988 New issues	150 M$ US	909
Exchange differences		72
Changes in composition (Ranchmen's)	21 M$ Can	105
Balance at 31 December 1988		1 620

10. CHANGES IN SHAREHOLDERS' FUNDS AND MINORITY INTERESTS

Shareholders' funds have increased by 1 513 MF and minority interest by 914 MF.

(MF)

	Shareholders' funds	Minority interest
Balance at 31 December 1987 (before allocation)	20 301	2 717
MOVEMENTS DURING THE YEAR		
TOTAL CFP share of 1987 result	1 316	-
Dividends paid relating to 1987	- 725	- 125
Increase in capital	17	319
Difference on conversion of foreign subsidiaries' balance sheets	1 062	156
Write-backs from revaluation reserves	- 33	- 4
Changes in the composition of the Group, purchase of minority interests and others	- 124	91
Share of minority interest in 1988 result	-	477
TOTAL MOVEMENTS	1 513	914
Balance at 31 December 1988	21 814	3 631

At 31 December 1987, the issued share capital of TOTAL CFP was made up of 36 247 279 shares of 50 F each, totalling 1 812 MF. In 1988, it was increased by 4 MF by the conversion of 7.5 % Convertible Loan Notes from 1979, representing 75 034 shares, and the exercise of options to subscribe for shares granted to Group employees, representing 3 896 shares.
The issued share capital at 31 December 1988 is made up, therefore, of 36 326 209 shares of 50 F each, totalling 1 816 MF.

NOTES

11. PROVISION FOR DEFERRED TAXATION

The provision for deferred taxation at 31 December 1988 has increased to 4 541 MF, as compared with 4 112 MF at 31 December 1987.

- Analysis by type (MF)

	31/12/88	31/12/87 restated
- Accelerated fiscal depreciation exploration/production assets ..	4 325	3 962
- Adjustment on consolidation and accounting for temporary differences	271	178
- Effect of taxable profit on provisions for deferred taxes by French subsidiaries	- 55	- 28
TOTAL	4 541	4 112

- Analysis of movements during the year : (MF)

Balance at 31/12/87	4 112
Charge for 1988	26
Exchange difference	403
	4 541

12. PROVISIONS FOR PENSIONS AND SIMILAR OBLIGATIONS

(MF)

Balance at 31/12/87 after restatement	4 123
Movements during the year	- 168
Balance at 31/12/88	3 955

The movements for the year are made up principally of provisions written back in accordance with the settlements in respect of 1988, and of a charge of 85 MF provided, as a matter of prudence, by TOTAL Compagnie Française des Pétroles to take account of a new severance plan whose details will not have been finalized until the first half of 1989.

13. PROVISIONS FOR OTHER LIABILITIES AND CHARGES

(MF)

	31/12/88	31/12/87 restated
Specific sector risks	975	1 370
Industrial, commercial and financial risks	2 029	1 902
TOTAL	3 004	3 272

14. LONG-TERM BORROWINGS

ANALYSIS BY MATURITY	31/12/88	
	(MF)	%
1990	1 340	9
1991	1 357	9
1992	2 457	17
1993	1 706	11
1994 and following years	8 155	54
TOTAL	15 015	100

This item does not include TOTAL CFP's short-term borrowings on medium-term lines of credit. They amounted to 2 655 MF at 31 December 1988 against 2 321 MF in 1987 and are included in short-term loans.

ANALYSIS BY CURRENCY	31/12/88		31/12/87 restated	
	(MF)	%	(MF)	%
French franc	6 196	41	5 976	48
US dollar	7 322	49	4 200	34
Pound sterling	919	6	1 694	14
Swiss franc	169	1	180	1
Others	409	3	296	3
TOTAL	15 015	100	12 346	100

This analysis includes long-term and medium-term currency debt exposure covered by transactions in the money market.

(MF)

ANALYSIS BY TYPE	31/12/88	31/12/87 restated
Debenture loans	6 152	5 131
Obligations under finance leases	1 524	1 080
Other borrowings	7 339	6 135
TOTAL	15 015	12 346

15. TURNOVER

ANALYSIS BY ACTIVITY	1988	1987 restated
Crude oil	12 965	15 277
Gas	4 259	3 639
Petroleum products - France	22 017	23 406
Petroleum products - Foreign	32 388	33 951
Others : - Chemicals	7 721	6 402
- Coal/Minerals/Solar energy	1 067	1 410
Services and other charges	2 873	2 658
TOTAL	83 290	86 743

GEOGRAPHICAL ANALYSIS		
France	27 397	29 384
Foreign	55 893	57 359
TOTAL	83 290	86 743

16. OPERATING EXPENSES

(MF)

	1988	1987 restated
Cost of sales	70 750	75 755
Dry hole expenditure	1 139	859
Net provisions for production-sharing agreements	133	- 139
Net provisions for operating expenses	- 424	126
TOTAL	71 598	76 601

17. TRANSFERS TO DEPRECIATION

(MF)

ANALYSIS BY TYPE	1988	1987 restated
Depreciation of goodwill	134	28
Other depreciation	4 690	3 651
TOTAL	4 824	3 679

ANALYSIS BY SECTOR OF OPERATION		
Petroleum exploration/production	2 361	1 275
Transport/refining/marketing	1 769	1 592
Chemicals	257	212
Coal/Minerals/Solar energy	266	483
Other	171	117
TOTAL	4 824	3 679

18. FINANCIAL INCOME

(MF)

	1988	1987 restated
Dividends received from non-consolidated affiliates	295	311
Other financial income	1 540	1 385
TOTAL	1 835	1 696

19. TAXATION

(MF)

	1988	1987 restated
Current taxes		
. on profits*	5 189	6 003
. on distribution	78	99
Deferred tax	26	226
TOTAL	5 293	6 328

* including taxes paid to oil producing countries.

20. OTHER EXPENSES AND INCOME

(MF)

	1988	1987 restated
Profit or loss on exchange	-	- 43
Gains and losses on asset disposals	550	1 614
Net financial provisions	292	- 305
Exceptional provisions	329	- 234
Other exceptional profits and losses	- 197	192
TOTAL	974	1 224

(Expenses are shown with a minus sign)

Gains and losses on disposals of assets include, in particular, the gain realized by TOP(NA) on disposal of its exploration and production assets in the United States for 146 MF and the gain realized by the OFP group in its share dealing activities amounting to 144 MF.

21. RESEARCH AND DEVELOPMENT

Group research and development expenses were 653 MF in 1988 and 600 MF in 1987. They have been charged as expenses.

NOTES

22. GROUP STAFF AND STAFF COSTS

GROUP STAFF		1988	1987
FRANCE	Executives	4 022	4 055
	Other employees	15 351	15 908
Sub-total FRANCE		19 373	19 963
FOREIGN	Executives	3 067	2 369
	Other employees	12 921	11 614
Sub-total outside France		15 988	13 983
GRAND TOTAL		35 361	33 946

This analysis is based on the number of employees at 31 December. Only employees of fully consolidated subsidiaries are included.

	1988	1987
STAFF COSTS (MF) (including social security and similar costs)	7 639	7 600

These amounts include the Group's share of the staff costs of joint interest and jointly controlled companies consolidated using the proportional method.

23. MANAGEMENT REMUNERATION

Remuneration paid as directors' fees and executive salaries to members of the parent company for their services in Group companies amounted to 2.4 MF in 1988.

24. CONTINGENT LIABILITIES

(MF)

GUARANTEES GIVEN	31/12/88	31/12/87 restated
. Bills discounted and not yet due	275	234
. In favour of customs authorities	6 655	6 210
. Loans to subsidiaries not fully consolidated	1 407	1 288
. Leasing operations	85	301
. Other	1 531	2 854
TOTAL	9 953	10 887
GUARANTEES RECEIVED	2 867	3 864

25. SEGMENTAL INFORMATION

Analysis of funds generated from operations and of the consolidated result.

The following tables provide an analysis of funds generated from operations, consolidated results and the stock holding effect in the refining and distribution sector.

The item "Chemicals" includes the Hutchinson group, and the item "Other sectors" relates only to interests in financial institutions, the most important of which are the Omnium Financier de Paris, Paribas and the Compagnie Générale de Géophysique.

Transfers between sectors, in particular between the petroleum production and the refining sectors, are taken at prices approximating market price.

(MF)

	1988				1987 (restated)			
	Funds generated from ope- rations	Consolidated result			Funds generated from ope- rations	Consolidated result		
		Group	Minorities	TOTAL		Group	Minorities	TOTAL
Petroleum exploration/production and trading								
- North sea	2 453	604	-	604	1 894	720	-	720
- Other areas	1 471	- 157	73	- 84	1 796	720	39	759
Sub-total	3 924	447	73	520	3 690	1 440	39	1 479
Refining/Marketing								
- France	732	12	-	12	466	- 643	- 238	- 881
- Other countries	1 517	386	214	600	1 521	987	- 34	953
Sub-total	2 249	398	214	612	1 987	344	- 272	72
Coal/Minerals/Solar energy	- 135	- 156	- 27	- 183	100	- 567	- 2	- 569
Chemicals	623	274	57	331	423	141	80	221
Other sectors	492	516	159	675	228	- 42	114	72
TOTAL	7 153	1 479	476	1 955	6 428	1 316	- 41	1 275

(MF)

ANALYSIS OF THE STOCK HOLDING EFFECT	1988		1987 (restated)	
	Group	Minorities	Group	Minorities
Refining/Marketing				
- France	- 540	- 20	100	50
- Other countries	- 40	-	20	50
TOTAL	- 580	- 20	120	100

FINANCIAL STATEMENTS OF TOTAL COMPAGNIE FRANÇAISE ═══════════ DES PETROLES (parent company)

GENERAL REPORT OF THE AUDITORS

Ladies and Gentlemen,

In accordance with our appointment at the Annual General Meeting on 20 June 1986, we present our report on :

- the audit of the annual accounts which are attached to this report,
- the specific confirmations and information required by law,

relating to the year ended 31 December 1988.

OPINION ON THE ANNUAL ACCOUNTS

We have audited the annual accounts by carrying out such procedures as we considered necessary in accordance with standards of the profession.

We certify that the annual accounts comply with the legal requirements and give a true and fair view of the result for the year and of the Company's financial position and assets at the end of the year.

SPECIFIC CONFIRMATIONS AND INFORMATION

We have performed specific examination procedures as required by law in accordance with the standards of the profession.

We are satisfied that the information included in the management report of the Board of Directors and in the documents addressed to the shareholders with regard to the financial position and the annual accounts is fairly presented and consistent with the annual accounts.

By enforcement of the articles 356 and 356-3 of the Companies Act of 24 July 1966, we confirm that the information relating to the investments and subsidiaries acquired during the year as well as the information relating to the identity of shareholders is correctly stated in the management report.

Paris, 20 April 1989

The Auditors
Members of Compagnie de Paris

CABINET CAUVIN, ANGLEYS, SAINT-PIERRE,
REVIFRANCE

FRINAULT-FIDUCIAIRE

F. ANGLEYS   R. AMIRKHANIAN

G. BARTHES de RUYTER   M. LEGER

SPECIAL REPORT OF THE AUDITORS

Ladies and Gentlemen,

In accordance with section 103 of the Companies Act of 24 July 1966, we hereby advise you of the agreements covered under section 101.

AGREEMENTS CONCLUDED DURING THE YEAR AFTER PRIOR APPROVAL

- Purchase of TOTAL Chimie

On 19 October 1988, your Board authorized the purchase by your Company of the 50 % interest owned by CRD TOTAL FRANCE in TOTAL Chimie. TOTAL CFP has bought 1 799 992 shares of TOTAL CHIMIE for an amount of French francs 1 511 993 280.

As a result of that transaction, TOTAL CFP now owns 100 % of TOTAL Chimie.

Directors of both companies :

Mr ORTOLI
Mr GRANIER de LILLIAC
Mr DENY
Mr GUILBAUD

- Waiver of a debt due from TOTAL Compagnie Minière

On 25 January 1989, your Board agreed to the waiving of a debt due from TOTAL Compagnie Minière for an amount of French francs 240 000 000.
This waiving concerns advances made to TOTAL Compagnie Minière from 1982 to 1988 and can be reversed under an earn-out provision.

Director of both companies :

Mr DENY

AGREEMENTS CONCLUDED IN PRIOR YEARS AND STILL EFFECTIVE DURING THE YEAR

- Cash agreement with CFP (Algérie)

On 4 November 1987, your Board has approved an additional clause to the cash agreement dated 1 February 1985, entered into with CFP (Algérie). This additional clause, applicable as of 1 July 1987, provides that the cash deposit from CFP (Algérie) to your Company will no longer bear interest and that the possibility of current account advances to CFP (Algérie) no longer exists.

Directors of both companies :

Mr DENY
Mr VAILLAUD

- Cash agreement with TOTAL Indonésie

The cash agreement between TOTAL CFP and TOTAL Indonésie, renewed on 5 November 1988, has been effective during the whole year. TOTAL Indonésie may, at its discretion, make unlimited transfers to or from your Company in French francs.
These transactions are not interest-bearing.

Directors of both companies :

Mr DENY
Mr VAILLAUD

- Participating loan to CRD TOTAL FRANCE

The agreement, dated 27 December 1985, defines the conditions of payment of interest relating to the participating loan of French francs 250 000 000 to CRD TOTAL FRANCE, for a period of 12 years.

The annual interest is made up of two elements : fixed interest and supplementary interest varying with the profits of CRD TOTAL FRANCE.

The interest income relating to this loan for the year 1988 amounted to French francs 14 836 250.

Directors of both companies :

Mr ORTOLI
Mr GRANIER de LILLIAC
Mr DENY
Mr GUILBAUD

- Agreement with CRD TOTAL FRANCE

The joint venture company owned equally with CRD TOTAL FRANCE for carrying out industrial research into refining and petrochemicals, incurred costs of French francs 120 835 880 for TOTAL CFP for the year 1988.

Directors of both companies :

Mr ORTOLI
Mr GRANIER de LILLIAC
Mr DENY
Mr GUILBAUD

- Non interest-bearing guarantee agreements

The non interest-bearing guarantee agreements, approved in prior years, were still effective in 1988 under the same conditions :

Company	Balance outstand-ing at 31.12.88	Percentage by your Company	Amount of guarantee given by your Com-pany at 31.12.88
. TOTAL CHIMIE			
Long term loan Crédit National 1973	6 250 000	50	3 125 000
. CRD TOTAL FRANCE			
Long term loan Crédit National 1980	16 800 000	100	16 800 000

Directors of both companies :

Mr ORTOLI
Mr GRANIER de LILLIAC
Mr DENY
Mr GUILBAUD

· **Modification to the retirement conditions offered to a director**

The modification of the Company's retirement plan conditions offered upon retirement to Mr DENY, Vice-Président Directeur Général, in accordance with a decision of the Board of Directors on 28 September 1984, is still applicable.

In addition, as in prior years, ordinary transactions carried out under normal conditions have occurred with businesses in which certain members of your Board of Directors have interests, or hold positions of responsibility.

Paris, 20 April 1989

The Auditors
Members of Compagnie de Paris

CABINET CAUVIN, ANGLEYS, SAINT-PIERRE,
REVIFRANCE

FRINAULT-FIDUCIAIRE

F. ANGLEYS   R. AMIRKHANIAN

G. BARTHES de RUYTER   M. LEGER

BALANCE SHEET AT 31 DECEMBER, 1988
(F.'000)

ASSETS

	31 December, 1988			31 December, 1987
	Gross Amounts	Depreciation and provisions	Net Amounts	Net Amounts
FIXED ASSETS	33 973 795	16 999 527	16 974 268	11 895 618
Intangible assets	241 492	240 888	604	604
Tangible assets	809 070	250 301	558 769	564 733
Land	230 922		230 922	232 633
Buildings	109 696	14 734	94 962	93 737
Other tangible assets	468 452	235 567	232 885	238 363
Financial assets	32 923 233	16 508 338	16 414 895	11 330 281
Shares in affiliated companies	17 637 420	6 206 390	11 431 030	7 136 955
Loans to affiliated companies	14 601 103	10 301 948	4 299 155	3 376 595
Other loans	681 719		681 719	810 402
Deposits	2 991		2 991	6 329
CURRENT ASSETS	11 864 743	12 885	11 851 858	14 335 208
Stocks	20 028	462	19 566	68 032
Debtors	10 967 412	12 423	10 954 989	12 702 440
Trade debtors	4 244 019	10 875	4 233 144	4 723 181
Other debtors	6 723 393	1 548	6 721 845	7 979 259
Marketable securities	737 517		737 517	1 428 804
Liquid assets	104 132		104 132	116 865
Regularization accounts	35 654		35 654	19 067
Prepayments	35 654		35 654	19 067
Deferred expenditure	21 697	8 351	13 346	19 733
Premiums on redeemable bonds	25 921	25 921	-	-
Difference on exchange	443 156		443 156	701 471
TOTAL	46 329 312	17 046 684	29 282 628	26 952 030

LIABILITIES

	31 December, 1988		31 December, 1987	
	Before AGM decisions	After AGM decisions (1)	Before AGM decisions	After AGM decisions
CAPITAL AND RESERVES	16 369 540	15 643 017	16 123 153	15 398 208
Issued capital	1 816 310	1 816 310	1 812 364	1 812 364
Share premium account : shares and converted bonds	2 970 721	2 970 721	2 958 579	2 958 579
Revaluation reserve	1 030 331	1 030 331	1 097 033	1 097 033
Legal reserve	181 236	181 632	180 404	181 236
Statutory reserves	23 046	23 046	23 046	23 046
Other reserves :				
. General reserves	8 586 000	8 876 000	7 826 000	8 586 000
. Surplus arising on exchange of shares	14 335	14 335	14 335	14 335
Profit brought forward	725 165	730 632	829 304	725 165
Profit for the year	1 022 386	-	1 381 638	-
Legal revaluation special provision	10	10	450	450
PROVISIONS FOR RISKS AND CHARGES	2 280 300	2 280 300	2 434 300	2 434 300
Provisions for financial risks	6 300	6 300	6 300	6 300
Provisions for pensions and similar commitments	1 254 000	1 254 000	1 058 000	1 058 000
Provisions for specific sectors risks	1 020 000	1 020 000	1 370 000	1 370 000
CREDITORS	10 127 052	10 853 575	7 686 913	8 411 858
Financial	4 759 083	4 759 083	3 623 829	3 623 829
Convertible debenture loan	118 850	118 850	132 179	132 179
Other debenture loans	2 774 506	2 774 506	1 835 119	1 835 119
Other loans and finance debts	1 817 544	1 817 544	1 564 397	1 564 397
Bank accounts	48 183	48 183	92 134	92 134
Operating	5 361 985	6 088 508	4 056 126	4 781 071
Trade creditors	3 761 913	3 761 913	2 650 291	2 650 291
Other creditors	1 600 072	2 326 595	1 405 835	2 130 780
Regularization accounts	5 984	5 984	6 958	6 958
Accruals and deferred income	5 984	5 984	6 958	6 958
Difference on exchange	505 736	505 736	707 664	707 664
TOTAL	29 282 628	29 282 628	26 952 030	26 952 030

(1) Subject to approval of the resolutions to be put to the AGM on 12 June 1989.

PROFIT AND LOSS ACCOUNT
(F.'000)

EXPENSES

	1988		1987	
OPERATING EXPENSES		26 034 267		29 691 732
Cost of sales				
. Crude oil and petroleum products	25 983 772		29 714 606	
. Variation in stocks	50 495		- 22 874	
Supplies from third parties		2 660 845		2 876 594
. Raw materials	411 630		607 255	
. Variation in raw materials stocks	471		44 657	
. Materials and supplies purchased for resale	40 620		45 048	
. External services				
- Staff	1 347 802		1 361 614	
- Leasing	53 760		57 671	
- Other	806 562		760 349	
Taxes, duties and similar payments		16 090		17 202
Staff costs		142 087		217 798
Depreciation and provisions		526 851		301 893
. Fixed assets : depreciation	96 465		65 175	
. Current assets : provision	2 386		6 718	
. Pensions and similar commitments	428 000		230 000	
Other expenses		2 118		2 053
TOTAL OPERATING EXPENSES		29 382 258		33 107 272
FINANCIAL CHARGES		2 274 104		3 014 333
Depreciation and provisions	1 640 703		2 266 812	
Interest and similar charges	618 473		500 029	
Loss on exchange	-		237 460	
Loss on sale of listed investments	14 928		10 032	
EXTRAORDINARY CHARGES		358 604		1 841 101
Management operations	20 543		40 956	
Capital operations				
- Book value of fixed assets sold	36 461		1 123 369	
- Others	1 600		6 776	
Provisions for specific sector risks	300 000		670 000	
EMPLOYEES' PROFIT SHARING PLAN		29 219		36 133
TAXES (PAID TO VARIOUS GOVERNMENTS)		3 508 049		4 516 086
PROFIT FOR THE YEAR		1 022 386		1 381 638
TOTAL		36 574 620		43 896 563

INCOME

	1988		1987	
OPERATING INCOME				
Sales of goods	30 654 962		35 074 252	
Production income				
. Sales	471 169		597 074	
. Income from ancillary activities	1 350 151		1 459 465	
Total sales	32 476 282	32 476 282	37 130 791	37 130 791
Provisions written back		239 718		214 581
. For current assets	7 718		15 581	
. For pensions and similar commitments	232 000		199 000	
TOTAL OPERATING INCOME		32 716 000		37 345 372
FINANCIAL INCOME		3 088 462		3 691 583
Investments	1 672 415		1 753 228	
Loans to affiliated companies	275 797		211 953	
Other interest	147 782		220 638	
Provisions written back and depreciation ...	908 962		1 469 377	
Profit on exchange	42 951		-	
Profit on sale of listed investments	40 555		36 387	
EXTRAORDINARY INCOME		770 158		2 859 608
Management operations	12 939		25 848	
Capital operations				
. Proceeds on sale of fixed assets	52 796		1 147 445	
. Other	54 423		85 901	
Provisions written back				
. For depreciation	-		1 100 414	
. For specific sector risks	650 000		500 000	
TOTAL		36 574 620		43 896 563

Extract from the Annual Report of AEG, 1988

Consolidated Balance Sheet of AEG Group as of December 31, 1988

Assets

	Notes	Dec. 31, 1988		Dec. 31, 1987	
		Million DM	Million DM	Million DM	Million DM
Fixed and Financial Assets					
Intangible Assets	(7)	539		27	
Fixed Assets	(8)				
Cost of acquisition or production		6,624		5,368	
Accumulated depreciation		− 4,290		− 3,589	
		2,334		1,779	
Financial Assets	(9)	305		178	
			3,178		1,984
Current Assets					
Inventories	(10)				
Total		3,491		3,070	
Payments received on account		− 1,628		− 1,632	
		1,863		1,438	
Receivables and Other Assets	(11)				
Trade receivables		2,509		2,433	
Receivables from affiliated companies		60		39	
Other receivables and current assets		418		344	
		2,987		2,816	
Marketable Securities/Certificates of Indebtedness	(12)	244		414	
Cash Items		1,088		1,171	
			6,182		5,839
Prepaid Expenses			16		9
			9,376		7,832

Shareholders' Equity and Liabilities

	Notes	Dec. 31, 1988		Dec. 31, 1987	
		Million DM	Million DM	Million DM	Million DM
Equity					
Subscribed capital		931		931	
Capital reserves		885		885	
Revenue reserves	(13)	86		57	
Net profit of AEG Aktiengesellschaft		9		−	
Minority interests	(14)	78		57	
			1,989		1,930
Special Untaxed Reserves	(15)		5		3
Accruals	(16)				
Accruals for pensions and similar obligations		2,679		2,497	
Other accruals		1,851		1,723	
			4,530		4,220
Financial Liabilities	(17)		598		347
Other Liabilities	(18)				
Trade payables		1,068		788	
Payables to a affiliated companies		582		67	
Other liabilities		604		477	
			2,254		1,332
			9,376		7,832

Consolidated Statement of Income of AEG Group
for the Period January 1 — December 31, 1988

	Notes	1988		1987	
		Million DM	Million DM	Million DM	Million DM
Sales	(21)	**13,380**		**11,660**	
Change in inventories and own work capitalized	(22)	+ 377		+ 276	
Total Operating Performance			**13,757**		**11,936**
Other operating income	(23)	+ 510		+ 533	
Cost of materials	(24)	− 6,153		− 5,376	
Personnel expenses	(25)	− 5,282		− 4,642	
Depreciation of intangible and fixed assets	(26)	− 484		− 357	
Other operating expenses	(27)	− 2,244		− 2,050	
Investment results (net)	(28)	+ 7		+ 16	
Interest income (net)	(29)	+ 23		+ 26	
Result from other financial investments and current assets securities (net)	(30)	− 3		− 3	
			− 13,626		− 11,853
Results from Ordinary Business Activity			+ 131		+ 83
Extraordinary results	(31)	− 4		− 19	
Taxes on income	(32)	− 33		− 16	
Other taxes	(32)	− 67		− 48	
			− 104		− 83
Net Income			27		−
Withdrawals from transfers to revenue reserves	(33)	− 18		+ 5	
Minority interest in income and losses	(33)	± 0		− 5	
Group Result			**9**		−

Report of the Board of Management

Consolidated Balance Sheet of AEG Aktiengesellschaft as of December 31, 1988

Assets

	Notes	Dec. 31, 1988		Dec. 31, 1987	
		Million DM	Million DM	Million DM	Million DM
Fixed and Financial Assets					
Intangible Assets	(7)	40		18	
Fixed Assets	(8)				
Cost of acquisition or production		605		329	
Accumulated depreciation		− 81		− 40	
		524		289	
Financial Assets	(9)	2,546		1,996	
			3,110		2,303
Current Assets					
Inventories	(10)				
Total		1,709		1,731	
Payments received on account		− 1,165		− 1,296	
		544		435	
Receivables and Other Assets	(11)				
Trade Receivables		1,180		1,308	
Receivables from affiliated companies		669		543	
Other receivables and current assets		199		177	
		2,048		2,028	
Marketable Securities/Certificates of Indebtedness	(12)	185		367	
Cash Items		887		1,055	
			3,664		3,885
Prepaid Expenses			3		1
			6,777		6,189

Shareholders' Equity and Liabilities

	Notes	Dec. 31, 1988		Dec. 31, 1987	
		Million DM	Million DM	Million DM	Million DM
Equity					
Subscribed capital		931		931	
Capital reserves (statutory reserve)		885		885	
Revenue reserves	(13)	344		344	
Net profit		9		−	
			2,169		2,160
Accruals	(16)				
Accruals for pensions and similar obligations		1,634		1,597	
Other accruals		991		1,080	
			2,625		2,677
Financial Liabilities	(17)		257		197
Other Liabilities	(18)				
Trade payables		573		495	
Payables to affiliated companies		887		450	
Other liabilities		266		210	
			1,726		1,155
			6,777		6,189

Consolidated Statement of Income of AEG Aktiengesellschaft
for the Period January 1 — December 31, 1988

	Notes	1988		1987	
		Million DM	Million DM	Million DM	Million DM
Sales	(21)	**7,133**		**7,232**	
Change in inventories and own work capitalized	(22)	+ 170		+ 205	
Total Operating Performance			**7,303**		**7,437**
Other operating income	(23)	+ 481		+ 333	
Cost of materials	(24)	− 3,446		− 3,513	
Personnel expenses	(25)	− 2,744		− 2,774	
Depreciation of intangible and fixed assets	(26)	− 65		− 181	
Other operating expenses	(27)	− 1,421		− 1,288	
Investment results (net)	(28)	− 104		− 45	
Interest income (net)	(29)	+ 33		+ 58	
Result from other financial investments and current assets securities (net)	(30)	− 1		− 1	
			− 7,267		− 7,411
Results from Ordinary Business Activity			+ 36		+ 26
Extraordinary result	(31)	−	± 0		
Taxes on income	(32)	− 6		− 2	
Other taxes	(32)	− 21		− 24	
			− 27		− 26
Net profit			9		−

Combined Notes

(1) Application of the new accounting legislation
The financial statements of the AEG Group and AEG Aktiengesellschaft were prepared according to the new accounting rules. To provide a clearer overview some individual items in the balance sheet and in the statement of income are grouped together. A breakdown is provided in the notes. All values are in million German marks (DM).

(2) Consolidated companies
In addition to the AEG Aktiengesellschaft, the AEG Group's financial statements consolidate 50 domestic and 94 foreign affiliates. In comparison with the preceding year, 8 domestic and 21 foreign affiliates have been consolidated for the first time. Four domestic and one foreign affiliate were no longer consolidated.

An additional 60 domestic and foreign affiliates were not consolidated because they were companies holding pension funds whose assets are subject to restrictions, or companies with little or no business activity. Total sales of these companies were less than 0.5% of the published sales of the group.

Seven associated companies were consolidated using the equity method of accounting. This method was not used for other associated companies because of immateriality.

(3) Affiliated companies and investments
The *affiliated companies* and *major investments* are listed on page 54 to 59 of this report.

A complete listing of holdings is on record at the district courts of Charlottenburg (Berlin) and Frankfurt.

(4) Principles of consolidation
Capital consolidation is performed using the "book value method". Under this method, the book values of the affiliated companies are netted against the underlying equity in these companies at the time of acquisition or initial consolidation. Arising differences are allocated to the book values of assets and liabilities of the affiliates, in so far as their market values of acquisition or initial consolidation deviate from the book values. Remaining positive or negative differences are netted and shown either as goodwill or disclosed as a reduction from reserves. The interests of minority shareholders of consolidated affiliates are recorded as "minority interests".

The book value method was also used for the *equity valuation* of associated companies. If the initial consolidation results in a debit difference this is booked against capital reserves or amortized in subsequent years, while a credit difference is reflected in the investment.

Intercompany receivables and payables as well as *income and expenses* are eliminated in consolidation. Results from sales within the group of products and services are eliminated from consolidated earnings. A *tax accrual* resulting from consolidation is offset by deferred income taxes.

(5) Foreign currency translation
In the individual financial statements currency values are translated at acquisition costs or at the lower bid price at year-end in case of receivables, or the higher selling price at year-end in case of payables.

In the AEG Group's financial statements, the fixed and financial assets of foreign affiliates are translated at the median currency exchange rate in effect at the year-end of the year of acquisition. The other assets and liabilities are translated at the median currency exchange rate in effect at the end of the current year. The difference in translation is included in the Group's capital reserves.

In the statement of income, revenue and expense items of these companies are translated at the average exchange rates of the current year. Exceptions are the depreciation of fixed and financial assets and gains and losses on the disposal of fixed and financial assets, which are translated at the rates in effect at acquisition. Profits and losses for the year are translated at the median exchange rate in effect at the balance sheet date. The difference arising from translating at the average rate for the year and the rate in effect at year-end is included under other operating income or expenses.

(6) Principles of classification and valuation
The individual statements included in the consolidated financial statements are prepared in accordance with the German accounting classification and valuation standards applicable to AEG Aktiengesellschaft.

Intangible assets are included at cost of acquisition and fixed assets at cost of acquisition or production, and in both instances they are valued excluding scheduled amortization and depreciation. The depreciation is calculated using uniform estimates of the assets' useful lives for the group.

Depreciation on buildings and factory and office equipment is calculated on a straight-line basis. Depreciation of *buildings* assume a maximum useful life of 40 years.

Depreciation for *other equipment, factory and office equipment* is based on the useful life anticipated for the different equipment categories. Assets of low value are fully depreciated in the year of acquisition.

Technical equipment and machines are depreciated in principle over a useful life of ten years on a declining balance basis, converting to straight-line depreciation as soon as this results in a higher charge.

From 1986 to 1988, to optimize taxes, AEG Aktiengesellschaft and AEG Olympia AG used straight-line depreciation for the additions to technical equipment and machines. Depreciation for assets of low value was based on a useful life of five years.

Investments in affiliated companies and *other investments* have been included at cost less write-downs to the lower actual value where the decrease in value is permanent.

Investments in associated companies in the AEG Group's financial statements are valued using the equity method.

Interest-free and low-interest-bearing *loans* are stated at their present values. In addition, allowances permissible under domestic tax regulations are deducted.

Raw materials and supplies, as well as *merchandise,* are valued at cost of acquisition or at a lower value, to the extent that it is economically required or permissible.

Finished goods and *work-in-progress,* as well as construction in progress, are valued at cost of production based on normal capacity utilization. Production costs include proportionate development and administrative overhead costs.

Profits and distribution expenses arising from intercompany trading are eliminated from inventories in consolidation for the financial statements of AEG Group.

According to the principle of loss-free valuation, all anticipated risks from slow-moving and obsolete inventories are covered by appropriate write-downs.

Receivables and *other assets* have been valued after providing for all known risks. Interest-free and low-interest claims maturing in more than one year are stated at their present value. In addition, the collection risk is covered by a general allowance for doubtful accounts.

Marketable securities are valued at the lower of cost or market value at year-end.

Pensions and *similar obligations* are valued according to Section 6a of the German Income Tax Code. An interest rate of 4% is used for Berlin facilities of AEG KABEL Group. Death benefit obligations are included in this item for the first time.

All anticipated risks are taken into account for the valuation of *other accruals.* Anniversary bonuses were not accrued. They amount to DM 150 million.

Deferred taxes for timing differences between tax and financial statements are reflected using the liability method and netted on the balance sheet.

Liabilities were valued at the repayment amount.

(7) Intangible assets
Additions to *intangible assets* include goodwill of recently consolidated companies amounting to DM 489 million. The remaining additions amounting to DM 44 million comprise patents and similar rights acquired from third parties, as well as software. A breakdown is provided on page 48.

(8) Fixed assets
Investments in *fixed assets* amount to DM 1,123 million. The development is shown on page 48.

(9) Financial assets
Additions to *financial assets* amounted to DM 191 million. Goodwill amounting to DM 34 million is included in the book values of associated companies valued for the first time using the equity method. The development is provided on page 48.

143

Development of Assets of AEG Group

(Million DM)	Acquisition, Production Costs					Depreciation		Book Value	
	Balance Dec. 31, 1987	Additions	Disposals	Transfers	Balance Dec. 31, 1988	Accu-mulated	1988	Dec. 31, 1988	Dec. 31, 1987
Intangible Assets	68	533	3	—	598	59	(19)	539	27
Fixed Assets									
Land, land rights and buildings including buildings on third party land	1,351	213	114	+ 40	1,490	593	(47)	897	754
Technical equipment and machines	2,710	343	138	+ 69	2,984	2,254	(173)	730	509
Other equipment, factory and office equipment	1,713	313	161	+ 25	1,890	1,443	(245)	447	375
Payments on account and assets under construction	142	254	2	− 134	260	—	(−)	260	141
	5,916	1,123	415	—	6,624	4,290	(465)	2,334	1,779
Financial Assets									
Shares in affiliated companies	48	6	2	+ 1	53	6	(−)	47	42
Shares in associated companies	70	90	56	—	104	2	(−)	102	65
Other investments	59	14	4	—	69	5	(−)	64	54
Securities	6	3	—	—	9	—	(−)	9	6
Loans	14	78	2	− 1	89	6	(3)	83	11
	197	191	64	—	324	19	(3)	305	178
	6,181	1,847	482	—	7,546	4,368	(487)	3,178	1,984

Development of Assets of AEG Aktiengesellschaft

(Million DM)	Acquisition, Production Costs					Depreciation		Book Value	
	Balance Dec. 31, 1987	Additions	Disposals	Transfers	Balance Dec. 31, 1988	Accu-mulated	1988	Dec. 31, 1988	Dec. 31, 1987
Intangible Assets	26	35	1	—	60	20	(13)	40	18
Fixed Assets									
Land, land rights and buildings including buildings on third party land	199	29	87	+ 11	152	21	(6)	131	177
Technical equipment and machines	1	67	1	+ 42	109	4	(4)	105	1
Other equipment, factory and office equipment	43	128	9	+ 18	180	56	(42)	124	25
Payments on account and assets under construction	86	150	1	− 71	164	—	(−)	164	86
	329	374	98	—	605	81	(52)	524	289
Financial Assets									
Shares in affiliated companies	2,018	658	113	+ 51	2,614	130	(−)	2,484	1,888
Investments	102	1	—	− 51	52	1	(−)	51	101
Loans	8	5	1	—	12	1	(−)	11	7
	2,128	664	114	—	2,678	132	(−)	2,546	1,996
	2,483	1,073	213	—	3,343	233	(65)	3,110	2,303

(10) Inventories

(Million DM)	AEG Group		AEG	
	Dec. 31, 1988	Dec. 31, 1987	Dec. 31, 1988	Dec. 31, 1987
Raw materials and supplies	570	482	270	259
Work-in-progress	809	672	354	310
Finished goods and merchandise	1,046	888	377	359
Constructions in progress	910	831	571	632
Payments on account	156	197	137	171
	3,491	3,070	1,709	1,731
– Payments received on account	– 1,628	– 1,632	– 1,165	– 1,296
	1,863	1,438	544	435

Payments on account were made under long-term purchase agreements and for deliveries and services from subcontractors in conjunction with major contracts. *Payments received on account* from customers are fully deducted from inventories.

(11) Receivables and other assets

(Million DM)	AEG Group		AEG	
	Dec. 31, 1988	Dec. 31, 1987	Dec. 31, 1988	Dec. 31, 1987
Trade receivables	2,509	2,433	1,180	1,308
(of which maturing in more than 1 year)	(143)	(148)	(73)	(109)
Receivables from affiliated companies	60	39	669	543
(of which maturing in more than 1 year)	(–)	(–)	(–)	(59)
Receivables from participations	30	26	27	19
(of which maturing in more than 1 year)	(–)	(–)	(–)	(–)
Other current assets	388	318	172	158
(of which maturing in more than 1 year)	(60)	(59)	(22)	(47)
	2 987	2 816	2 048	2 028

Receivables include respective notes receivable.

Receivables from affiliated companies relate to domestic and foreign affiliates of the AEG Group which have not been consolidated due to immateriality, as well as receivables from Daimler-Benz AG and its affiliated companies.

Other current assets consist of receivables other than those resulting from normal business activity. This includes deferred interest income of DM 21 million.

(12) Marketable securities and certificates of indebtedness

(Million DM)	AEG Group		AEG	
	Dec. 31, 1988	Dec. 31, 1987	Dec. 31, 1988	Dec. 31, 1987
Marketable securities	94	33	47	6
Certificates of indebtedness	150	381	138	361
	244	414	185	367

These items represent an interest-earning liquid asset.

(13) Revenue reserves
The Group's *revenue reserves* include those of AEG Aktiengesellschaft as well as the Group's interest in respective reserves and in the income and loss of consolidated companies. Differences not shown as goodwill at the initial consolidation and the profits resulting from consolidation are also included. DM 18 million of the net income of the Group was added to the revenue reserves.

(14) Minority interests
This item consists of the interests of outside shareholders in equity, principally at AEG Westinghouse Transport-Systeme Beteiligungsgesellschaft mbH (Berlin), AEG ETI Elektrik Endüstrisi A.Ş. (Istanbul), and AEG Austria Gesellschaft m.b.H. (Wien).

(15) Special untaxed reserves

The *special untaxed reserves* contain principally the net difference according to Section 52, (5), of the German Income Tax Code.

(16) Accruals

Accruals for pensions and similar obligations in 1988 have been increased by the full amount of the statutory contribution for the year. The total amount of obligations not reflected in the balance sheet amount to DM 106 million. This constitutes about 4% of the respective balance sheet item.

Other accruals include the following:

(Million DM)	AEG Group		AEG	
	Dec. 31, 1988	Dec. 31, 1987	Dec. 31, 1988	Dec. 31, 1987
Accruals	1,808	1,705	986	1,076
Tax accruals	43	18	5	4
	1,851	1,723	991	1,080

Expenses were accrued for warranties, potential losses from pending business, unbilled expenses for current year's sales, bonuses, and employee benefits. *Accruals for taxes* contain no deferred taxes, as these have been netted with the deferred tax assets.

(17) Financial liabilities

(Million DM)	AEG Group		AEG	
	Dec. 31, 1988	Dec. 31, 1987	Dec. 31, 1988	Dec. 31, 1987
Liabilities to banks	576	339	251	197
(of which due in				
– 1 year or less	(280)	(127)	(27)	(21)
– more than 5 years)	(118)	(73)	(92)	(80)
Other financial liabilities	22	8	6	–
(of which due in				
– 1 year or less	(2)	(2)	(3)	(–)
– more than 5 years)	(–)	(–)	(–)	(–)
	598	347	257	197

Liabilities to banks include loans at preferential interest rates associated with promotion of investment, regional development programs, the European Recovery Program (ERP), and export financing loans. *Other financial liabilities* arise primarily from the funding of foreign affiliates.

In the AEG Group, DM 364 million are collateralized by mortgages and accounts receivable; at AEG Aktiengesellschaft DM 100 million by mortgages and DM 5 million by accounts receivable.

(18) Other liabilities

(Million DM)	AEG Group		AEG	
	Dec. 31, 1988	Dec. 31, 1987	Dec. 31, 1988	Dec. 31, 1987
Trade payables	1,068	788	573	495
(of which due in 1 year or less)	(1,065)	(783)	(570)	(490)
Notes on bills accepted and drawn	31	19	–	–
(of which due in 1 year or less)	(31)	(19)	(–)	(–)
Payables to affiliated companies	582	67	887	450
(of which due in				
– 1 year or less	(582)	(65)	(887)	(449)
– more than 5 years)	(–)	(1)	(–)	(–)
Payable to participations	12	22	7	10
(of which due in 1 year or less)	(12)	(22)	(7)	(10)
Other liabilities	561	436	259	200
(of which due in				
– 1 year or less	(546)	(427)	(256)	(193)
– more than 5 years)	(3)	(4)	(2)	(4)
(Tax portion)	(133)	(111)	(66)	(73)
(Social benefits portion)	(103)	(84)	(51)	(51)
	2,254	1,332	1,726	1,155

Payables to affiliated companies result from current business with the non-consolidated affiliates. This item also includes obligations to other affiliated companies of the Daimler-Benz Group. Also included are loans of DM 500 million. *Other liabilities* comprise obligations not resulting from trade.

Other liabilities collateralized by receivables amount to DM 16 million for AEG Group.

(19) Contingent liabilities

(million DM)	AEG Group		AEG	
	Dec. 31, 1988	Affiliated companies portion	Dec. 31, 1988	Affiliated companies portion
Liability on bills	97	(–)	20	(–)
Guarantees	152	(–)	331	(201)
Warranties	21	(–)	–	(–)
Securities for outside obligations	7	(–)	1	(–)
	277	(–)	352	(201)

(20) Other financial commitments

(Million DM)	AEG Group		AEG	
	Dec. 31, 1988	Affiliated companies	Dec. 31, 1988	Affiliated companies
Lease and rental obligations for real estate	613	(75)	439	(14)
Lease and rental obligations for equipment	178	(7)	846	(743)
	791	(82)	1 285	(757)

Other financial commitments are listed at their present value.

(21) Sales

Sales include customer billings for products and services, less price reductions, discounts, and special allowances. License income is included.

A breakdown of sales by geographic region and fields of activity is included in the report of the Board of Management on page 8.

(22) Change in inventories and own work capitalized

(Million DM)	AEG Group		AEG	
	1988	1987	1988	1987
Increase in inventories of finished goods, work-in-progress and constructions in progress	244	202	116	160
Own work capitalized	133	74	54	45
	377	276	170	205

(23) Other operating income

Other operating income includes income from the disposal of fixed assets, the release of accruals, and proceeds from sales of materials and scrap, special manufacturing allowances granted to manufacturers in Berlin, currency exchange gains, and other income not otherwise accounted for. In the income statement of AEG Aktiengesellschaft this item also comprises income resulting from allocation of certain taxes to affiliated companies and the portion of administrative overhead costs reimbursed by affiliated companies.
The consolidated revenue from elimination of special untaxed reserves amounts to DM 0.4 million for AEG Group.

(24) Cost of materials

(Million DM)	AEG Group		AEG	
	1988	1987	1988	1987
Cost of raw materials, supplies, and merchandise	5,913	5,185	3,373	3,439
Cost of purchased services	240	191	73	74
	6,153	5,376	3,446	3,513

(25) Personnel expenses

(Million DM)	AEG Group		AEG	
	1988	1987	1988	1987
Wages and salaries	4,276	3,742	2,242	2,263
Social security taxes and employee welfare expenses	737	641	366	366
Expenditures for old-age benefits	269	259	136	145
	5,282	4,642	2,744	2,774

The following is an overview of average employment level:

	AEG Group		AEG	
	1988	1987	1988	1987
Fields of Activity				
Power Engineering	7,902	7,805	2,258	2,138
Automation Systems	7,950	6,695	4,310	4,061
Transportation Systems	2,476	2,079	1,137	1,713
Office and Communication Systems	10,209	10,457	98	2,825
Aerospace and Defense Systems	11,268	11,639	9,787	9,293
Microelectronics	6,114	–	–	–
Electrical and Electronic Standard Products and Components	20,679	20,622	11,291	11,395
Electrical Consumer Products	11,020	10,498	7,583	7,086
Others	9,469	9,077	5,719	5,480
	87,087	78,872	42,183	43,991

(26) Depreciation of intangible and fixed assets

A detailed listing of depreciation is provided in the schedules development of assets of AEG Group and AEG Aktiengesellschaft on page 48. Extraordinary depreciation amounting to DM 24 million was taken by AEG Group in accordance with several tax regulations relating to the promotion of business in Berlin, research and development, and Section 6b and 7d of the German Income Tax Code.

(27) Other operating expenses

Other operating expenses include losses from disposal of fixed assets, losses from write-downs of current assets other than inventories, and expenses for outside services such as repairs, transportation, rents and leases, as well as expenses for travel, fees, contributions, and currency exchange losses. This item also reflects additions to and utilization of accruals for operating risks.

(28) Result from participations (net)

(Million DM)	AEG Group		AEG	
	1988	1987	1988	1987
Income from profit and loss transfer agreements with affiliated companies	3	2	13	30
Income from investments	2	12	58	52
(of which from affiliated companies)	(–)	(1)	(55)	(39)
Losses under profit and loss transfer agreements	–	–	– 175	– 127
Profit from associated companies	2	2	–	–
	7	16	– 104	– 45

Losses under profit and loss transfer agreements at AEG Aktiengesellschaft principally concern AEG Olympia AG and AEG KANIS GmbH.

(29) Interest income (net)

(Million DM)	AEG group		AEG	
	1988	1987	1988	1987
Interest and similar income	164	121	163	145
(of which from affiliated companies)	(8)	(–)	(72)	(54)
Interest and similar expenses	– 141	– 95	– 130	– 87
(of which from affiliated companies)	(– 6)	(–)	(– 60)	(– 51)
	23	26	33	58

(30) Result from other financial investments and current asset securities (net)

(Million DM)	AEG Group		AEG	
	1988	1987	1988	1987
Income from other securities and loans in financial assets	1	1	–	–
Write-downs of financial investments and marketable securities	– 4	– 4	– 1	– 1
	– 3	– 3	– 1	– 1

(31) Extraordinary result

(Million DM)	AEG Group		AEG	
	1988	1987	1988	1987
Extraordinary income	53	0	–	+ 92
Extraordinary expenses	– 57	– 19	–	– 92
Extraordinary result	– 4	– 19	–	± 0

The *extraordinary result* is almost even at a loss of DM 4 million. The income here results from the sale of the steam turbine operations in Nürnberg and from the sale of shares of a foreign affiliate. The extraordinary expenses relate primarily to restructuring costs in the Office and Communication Systems Division.

(32) Taxes

Income Taxes in Germany include corporate and local income taxes and abroad all foreign income taxes. Income tax credits on earnings from domestic affiliates have been netted in this item. No deferred tax expense is shown, since deferred tax income and expenses have been netted.

Other taxes principally comprise the property-related taxes on assets, net worth, and real estate.

(33) Allocations to and withdrawals from transfers to revenue reserves
Minority interest in income and losses

The net income and losses of the affiliated companies and the income effect of the consolidation were offset against the Group's revenue reserves. The Group result is shown in the same amount as the result of AEG Aktiengesellschaft.

Minority interests amount to DM 8 million in income and DM 8 million in losses.

(34) Relationship with parent company

Daimler-Benz Aktiengesellschaft, Stuttgart, with whom we have a company interlinking contract, is the parent company of AEG Aktiengesellschaft. The annual financial statement and report of AEG Group is consolidated into the annual financial Group statement and report of the parent company. This consolidated statement is filed with the Trade Register in Stuttgart.

(35) Remuneration received by Members of the Supervisory Board and the Board of Management
During 1988, remuneration was received by the Members of the Supervisory Board of AEG Aktiengesellschaft amounting to DM 387,000 and by Members of its Board of Management amounting to DM 6,230,000. Former Members of the Board of Management and their survivors received sums totaling DM 1,562,000.

Accruals for pensions for former Members of the Board of Management of AEG Aktiengesellschaft amount to DM 12,285,000.

The membership of the Supervisory Board and of the Board of Management is listed on pages 2 and 3.

Berlin and Frankfurt, March 6, 1989

AEG Aktiengesellschaft

The Board of Management

Based on our audit performed in accordance with our professional duties, the accounting records and the financial statements and the consolidated financial statements comply with legal regulations. The financial statements and the consolidated financial statements present, in compliance with required accounting principles, a true and fair view of the net worth, financial position and results of the company and the Group. The combined management and Group management report is in agreement with the financial statements and the consolidated financial statements.

Frankfurt, March 6, 1989

BDO Deutsche Warentreuhand Aktiengesellschaft
Wirtschaftsprüfungsgesellschaft

Dr. Jacob   Neukirchen
Auditor   Auditor

Appendix II

Other Summaries

Subsidiaries and Affiliated Companies (as of December 31, 1988)

Name of Company	Subscribed Capital Million DM	Ownership Share of the AEG Group (%)
Consolidated Domestic Subsidiaries		
Direct Subsidiaries of AEG Aktiengesellschaft		
AEG Anlagenvermietung GmbH & Co. Frankfurt oHG, Frankfurt am Main	1,801.00	100
AEG Olympia Aktiengesellschaft, Wilhelmshaven[1][2]	170.00	99.2
AEG Westinghouse Transport-Systeme Beteiligungsgesellschaft mbH, Berlin[4]	131.00	80.9
TELEFUNKEN electronic GmbH, Heilbronn[4]	93.75	98
AEG Elektrowerkzeuge GmbH, Winnenden	80.00	99.8
AEG KABEL Aktiengesellschaft, Mönchengladbach	57.60	98.3
AEG KANIS GmbH, Nürnberg[1][2]	55.00	100
DUOFROST Kühl- und Gefriergeräte GmbH, Wiesbaden[1][2]	20.00	100
Eltro GmbH Gesellschaft für Strahlungstechnik, Heidelberg	13.00	73.8
Sachsenwerk Aktiengesellschaft, Regensburg[2][3]	10.00	100
GEI-Gesellschaft für Elektronische Informationsverarbeitung mbH, Aachen	10.00	75
ELEKLUFT Elektronik- und Luftfahrtgeräte GmbH, Bonn	7.00	74
Lloyd Dynamowerke GmbH, Bremen[2]	7.00	100
DEBEG GmbH, Hamburg und Berlin	6.00	100
Elektro-Mechanik GmbH, Wenden[1][2]	6.00	100
Berliner Magnetbahn GmbH, Berlin[4]	4.00	100
Elektron Versorgungsverwaltung GmbH, Frankfurt am Main[1][2]	4.00	100
AEG Electrotecnica Construction GmbH, Frankfurt am Main[1][2]	2.32	100
Modular Computer GmbH, Konstanz	2.00	100
ATM Computer GmbH, Konstanz	1.00	100
GEI Software-Technik GmbH & Co. KG, Berlin	1.00	100
IFM Internationale Fluggeräte und Motoren GmbH, Weinheim	1.00	100
AEG Anlagenexportgesellschaft mbH, Frankfurt am Main[2]	0.50	100
PGS Planungsgesellschaft mbH Architekten Ingenieure, Frankfurt am Main[1][2]	0.50	100
EAS Assekuranz Vermittlungs-GmbH, Frankfurt am Main[1]	0.37	54.8
Werbeagentur Dr. Kuhl GmbH, Frankfurt am Main[2]	0.20	100
AEG Anlagenvermietung GmbH, Frankfurt am Main	0.05	100
GEI Software-Technik Verwaltungsgesellschaft mbH, Berlin	0.05	100
MODICON Automatisierungstechnik GmbH, Frankfurt am Main[4]	0.05	100
TELEFUNKEN Patentverwertungsgesellschaft mbH, Ulm[1][2]	0.05	100

[1] A dependency agreement exists with this company.
[2] A profit and loss transfer agreement exists with this company.
[3] This is an integrated company in accordance with Section 322 of the German Corporations Act (AEG Aktiengesellschaft jointly responsible for liabilities).
[4] Consolidated for the first time in this business year.

Name of Company	Subscribed Capital Million DM	Ownership Share of the AEG Group (%)
Indirect Subsidiaries of AEG Aktiengesellschaft		
AEG Westinghouse Transport-Systeme GmbH, Berlin[3])	90.00	80.9
EUROSIL electronic GmbH, Eching[1])[2])[3])	46.00	96
AEG Isolier- und Kunststoff GmbH, Kassel[1])[2])	16.00	97.6
Kupfer-Walzwerk Berlin GmbH, Berlin	3.00	49.2
Electrotecnica Construction GmbH, Frankfurt am Main[2])	2.30	100
Dekatra Transportgesellschaft mbH, Mönchengladbach	2.00	98.3
„HIRSCH" Kupfer- und Messingwerke GmbH, Mönchengladbach	2.00	98.3
Magnetbahn GmbH, Starnberg[1])[2])	1.25	61.5
Betefa Berliner Telefonschnur- und Spezialkabel-Fabrik GmbH, Berlin[2])	1.00	98.3
GEI Rechnersysteme GmbH, Aachen	1.00	45
BST Servo-Technik GmbH, Bielefeld	1.00	65
FABEG GmbH, Bretten[1])[2])	0.40	80.9
GEI Informatik GmbH, Stuttgart[3])	0.15	52.5
AEG Olympia System GmbH, Frankfurt am Main[3])	0.10	99.2
Olympia Leasing GmbH, Wilhelmshaven[1])[2])	0.05	99.2
BRV Beratungsgesellschaft für Risikovorsorge im industriellen Bereich mbH, Frankfurt am Main[2])	0.05	54.8
Kabelwerk Rheydt GmbH, Mönchengladbach[2])	0.05	98.3
Marine Elektronik Schiffselektronische Anlagen GmbH, Hamburg[2])	0.05	100
Modular Computer Systems GmbH, Hamburg[1])[2])	0.05	100
Vereinigte Draht- und Kabelwerke GmbH, Duisburg[2])	0.05	98.3

Domestic Non-Consolidated Companies

Affiliated with AEG Aktiengesellschaft		
AEG-Elotherm GmbH, Remscheid	15.00	50
Feinmechanische Werke Mainz GmbH, Mainz	9.00	25
Forbach GmbH, Bad Neustadt	3.30	50

[1]) A dependency agreement exists with this company.
[2]) A profit and loss transfer agreement exists with this company.
[3]) Consolidated for the first time in this business year.

Report of the Board of Management

Name of Company		Subscribed Capital in Local Currency (1,000)	Ownership Share of the AEG Group (%)
Consolidated Foreign Subsidiaries			
Direct Subsidiaries of AEG Aktiengesellschaft			
AEG International AG, Zürich	sfr	203,000	100
AEG Capital Corporation, New York (New York)[1]	US-$	157,842	100
Modular Computer Systems, Inc., Fort Lauderdale (Florida)	US-$	55,716	100
Modular Computer Services, Inc., Wokingham	US-$	11,655	100
Modular Computer Systems Ireland Ltd., Cork	Ir£	1,016	100
Modular Computer Holdings Ltd., Hamilton	Ir£	1,624	100
Modular Computer Systems Benelux B.V., Utrecht	hfl	200	100
MODCOMP Canada Ltd., Mississauga (Ontario)	kan$	120	100
MODCOMP France S.A.R.L., Rungis	FF	1,000	100
Olympia USA Inc., Somerville (New Jersey)	US-$	30,150	100
AEG Power Tool Corporation, New London (Connecticut)	US-$	9,040	100
AEG Corporation, Somerville (New Jersey)	US-$	5,500	100
MODICON, Inc., Andover (Massachusetts)[1]	US-$	137,432	100
Septor Electronics Corporation, El Paso (Texas)[1]	US-$	1,704	55
Suomen AEG Oy, Helsinki	Fmk	45,801	100
AEG Svenska AB, Solna	skr	30,000	100
AEG Hem & Hushall AB, Solna	skr	2,000	100
AEG Elektroverken AB, Gävle[1]	skr	150	100
AEG Hellas Viomichania Ilektrikon Kataskevon A.E., Moschaton (Athen)	Dr.	900,800	100
AEG Argentina S.A. I. y C., Buenos Aires	Å	47,100	100
Officine Galileo di Sicilia S.p.A., Milazzo (Messina)	Lit	2,000,000	100
Compagnia Generale Contatori — Co.Ge.Co. S.p.A., Mailand	Lit	1,260,000	100
AEG Servo Systems Ltd., Ennis[1]	Ir£	70	80
Eleven other companies			

[1] Consolidated for the first time in this business year.

Name of Company		Subscribed Capital in Local Currency (1,000)	Ownership Share of the AEG Group (%)
Subsidiaries of AEG International AG			
AEG Ibérica de Electricidad S.A., Madrid	Ptas	3,800,100	100
AEG Fábrica de Motores S.A., Terrassa (Barcelona)	Ptas	3,000,000	100
OTEMA S.A., Madrid	Ptas	346,000	100
AEG Austria Gesellschaft m.b.H., Wien	S	300,000	57
MODICON Handelsgesellschaft m.b.H., Wien[1]	S	2,000	57
AEG ETI Elektrik Endüstrisi A.Ş., Gebze (Istanbul)	TL.	30,000,000	50.6
AEG Italiana S.p.A., Cinisello Balsamo (Mailand)	Lit	20,800,000	100
MODICON Italiana S.r.l., Varese[1]	Lit	1,800,000	100
AEG France S.A., Clamart (Paris)	FF	68,000	100
MODICON France S.A.R.L., Montigny-le-Bretonneux[1]	FF	3,050	100
AEG (U.K.) Ltd., Slough	£	5,600	100
MODICON Electronics Ltd., Basingstoke[1]	£	1,100	100
AEG Finanz-Holding S.A., Luxemburg	sfr	15,000	100
S.A. belge AEG, Brüssel	bfrs	250,000	100
MODICON Belgium N.V., Deurne[1]	bfrs	1,300	100
AEG Nederland N.V., Amsterdam	hfl	11,000	100
MODICON Service B.V., Halfweg[1]	hfl	1,100	100
MODICON Nederland B.V., Maarssenbroek[1]	hfl	900	100
AEG Norge A/S, Oslo	nkr	30,000	100
AEG (Pty.) Ltd., Johannesburg	R	10,736	100
AEG Dansk Aktieselskab, Albertslund	dkr	20,000	100
AEG Bayly Inc., Ajax (Ontario)	kan$	3,291	100
TELEFUNKEN Rádio e Televisão Ltda., São Paulo/SP	Cz$	1,337,000	100
TELEFUNKEN da Amazônia S.A., Manaus/AM	Cz$	700,000	100
AEG do Brasil S.A., São Paulo/SP	Cz$	1,000,000	100
AEG Sistemas Industriais Ltda., São Paulo/SP	Cz$	320,000	100
Robotecnica S.r.l., Sesto San Giovanni (Mailand)	Lit	1,115,000	92.4
AEG Portuguesa S.A., Lissabon	Esc	100,800	99.8
AEG Luxembourg S.à r.l., Luxemburg	lfrs	25,000	75.2
AEG-Pakistan (Private) Limited, Karatschi	pR	10,000	60
AEG Venezolana S.A., Caracas	Bs.	7,500	70
AEG Hausgeräte AG, Schwerzenbach	sfr	270	100
AEG Genel Elektrik T.A.Ş., Istanbul	TL.	25,000	99

[1] Consolidated for the first time in this business year.

Name of Company		Subscribed Capital in Local Currency (1,000)	Ownership Share of the AEG Group (%)
Direct Subsidiaries of AEG Olympia Aktiengesellschaft			
Olympia France S.A., Clamart (Paris)	FF	69,000	99.2
TELTEC, S.A. de C.V., Mexiko, D.F.	mex$	16,567,000	99.2
Olympia de México, S.A. de C.V., Los Reyes	mex$	10,764,000	98.9
Olympia Mexicana, S.A. de C.V., Mexiko, D.F.	mex$	239,000	99.2
AEG Mexicana, S.A. de C.V., Mexiko, D.F.	mex$	2,502,000	99.2
Montajes y Reparaciones, S.A. de C.V., Puebla	mex$	6,000	99.2
Olympia Business Machines Co. Ltd., London	£	2,800	99.2
Olympia (Aust.) Pty. Ltd., Artarmon	$A	5,500	99.2
Olympia Italiana S.p.A., Cinisello Balsamo (Mailand)	Lit	6,030,000	99.2
Olympia (Chile) Ltda., Santiago de Chile	chil$	849,900	99.2
Olympia Business Machines Canada Ltd., Don Mills (Ontario)	kan$	3,800	99.2
Olympia Büromaschinen Ges.m.b.H., Salzburg	S	33,000	99.2
Olympia Máquinas de Oficina, S.A., Madrid	Ptas	200,000	99.2
Olympia Cataluña, S.A., Barcelona	Ptas	56,000	99.2
Olympia N.V. − S.A., Dilbeek	bfrs	55,000	99.2
Olympia Kontormaskiner A/S, Kopenhagen	dkr	7,200	99.2
Olympia Büromaschinen AG, Rümlang (Zürich)	sfr	1,500	99.2
Olympia (South Africa) (Pty.) Ltd., Johannesburg	R	2,200	99.2
Olympia Machines de Bureau S.A., Luxemburg	lfrs	26,000	99.2
Olympia Office Machines (H.K.) Ltd., Hongkong	HK$	2,600	99.2
AEG Olympia B.V., Den Haag[1])	hfl	12	99.2
Affiliated with Other Domestic Subsidiary Companies			
AEG Westinghouse Transportation Systems, Inc., Pittsburgh (Pennsylvania)[1])	US-$	20,000	80.9
TELEFUNKEN electronic Ges.m.b.H., Vöcklabruck[1])	S	52,000	98
TELEFUNKEN Semiconductors (Philippines) Inc., Manila[1])	P	38,624	98
Magnetic Transit of America, Inc., Los Angeles (Kalifornien)	US-$	50	64.7
Crossley & Bradley Ltd., Leyland	£	20	97.6
EUROSIL electronics Ltd., Hongkong[1])	HK$	10	96

[1]) Consolidated for the first time in this business year.

154

Name of Company		Subscribed Capital in Local Currency (1,000)	Ownership Share of the AEG Group (%)
Selected Non-Consolidated Foreign Subsidiaries and Affiliated Companies			
Affiliated with AEG Aktiengesellschaft			
Thomson Grand Public S.A., Paris	FF	2,673,300	2.5
NGEF Ltd., Bangalore	iR	100,000	22.6
AEG Pte. Ltd., Singapur	S$	5,000	95
Al-Jazirah Solar Energy Factory Ltd., Riad	S.Rls	3,250	26
Sager Electrical & Mechanical Company Ltd., Riad	S.Rls	2,000	40
AEG Japan Ltd., Tokio	Y	100,000	100
P.T. AEG-BINA, Jakarta	Rp.	392,830	51
Affiliated with AEG International AG			
Sherkate Sahami Kontorsazi Iran (Aam), Ghazvin	Rls.	1,035,000	8
Société Commerciale Immobilière Luxembourgeoise S.à r.l., Luxemburg	lfrs	21,000	89.6
Sherkate Sahami Khass AEG Iran, Teheran	Rls.	10,000	100
AEG China Ltd., Hongkong	HK$	200	100
AEG Colombiana Ltda., Bogotà	kol$	5,500	100
Others			
Siliconix Inc., Santa Clara (Kalifornien)	US-$	27,472	38.9
Sähköliikkeiden Oy, Vantaa	Fmk	29,700	20
SLO-Idman Oy, Mäntsälä	Fmk	18,000	49.9
Olympia Canarias, S.A., Teneriffa	Ptas	80,000	99.2
AEG Ilektroergalia A.E., Pal. Faliro (Athen)	Dr.	10,000	79.8
Eletromecânica e Hidráulica Ltda., Belo Horizonte/MG	Cz$	48,291	49

Glossary of Some Accounting Terms in English, Spanish, French and German

ENGLISH	SPANISH
A	
account	cuenta
accountancy, accounting	contabilidad
accountant	contable (also bookkeeper), experto
accounts (annual)	cuentas
annual general meeting	junta general
appropriation	apropriación
articles (of limited company)	articulos de asociación
assets	activo
associated company	participación
audit	revisión de cuentas
auditor	auditor, censor de cuentas
B	
balance (on an account)	saldo
balance sheet	balance de situación, balance
bank	banco
bearer (share)	acciones al portador
bill of exchange	lettre de cambio
board of directors	consejo de administración
bookkeeping	teneduría de libros
books of account	libros contables
borrowings	capital a préstamo
buildings	edificios
business	negocios

FRENCH	GERMAN
poste (bookkeeping), compte (eg bank)	Konto (bookkeeping), Kontokorrent (current account)
comptabilité	Buchführung, Rechnungslegung
comptable	Buchhalter
comptes annuels	Jahresanschluss
assemblée générale ordinaire	ordentliche Hauptversammlung
affectation	Gewinnverwendung
status	Gesellschaftsvertrag
éléments de l'actif	Vermögensgegenstanden, Aktiva (side of balance sheet)
participation	Beteiligung, Beteiligungsgesellschaft
révision	Prüfung
commissaire aux comptes	Prüfer, Wirtschaftsprüfer

solde	Saldo, Stand (fixed assets etc)
bilan	Bilanz
banque	Bank, Kreditinstitut
porteur (action au)	Inhaber (Aktie)
effet	Wechsel
conseil d'administration (managing), conseil de surveillance (supervisory), directoire (one-tier structure)	Vorstand (managing), Aufsichsrat (supervisory)
comptabilité, tenue des livres comptables	Buchhaltung
livres comptables	Buchführung
endettements (total), emprunt (loan payable)	Kreditaufnahmen
bâtiments, constructions, immeubles	Gebäude
affaires, enterprise	Geschäft

ENGLISH	SPANISH
C	
capital	capital
capital gain	plusvalía
capital loss	pérdida de capital
capitalise (expenses to assets)	capitalizar
cash at bank	caja
cash in hand, in cash	efectivo
cash flow	flujo de caja
chairman	presidente
chartered accountant	contandor habilitado
cheque	talón, cheque
Civil Code.	Código Civil
Commercial Code	Código de Comercio
company	sociedad, compañía, firma
consolidated	consolidado
contingent	contingencia
contract	contrato, convenio
conversion	conversión
convertible	convertible
corporation tax	impuesto sobre renta de la sociedad
cost (purchase cost)	costes, gastos
cost accounting	contabilidad analítica, contabilidad de costes, contabilidad industrial
costs	costes, gastos
credit	haber (bookkeeping), crédito
creditor	acreedor
currency	divisas
current assets	activo circulante, corriente
current value	valor corriente
current liabilities	pasivo circulante, corriente

FRENCH	GERMAN
capital	Kapital
plus-value	Veräusserungsgewinn, Kapital- zuwachs
moins-value	Kapitalverzehr
porter à l'actif	aktivieren
banques	Guthaben bei Kreditinstituten
caisse	Kasse, Kassenbestand
cash flow, autofinancement	cash flow, Finanzfluss
président, PDG	Vorsitzender
expert comptable (equivalent)	Wirtschaftsprüfer, Steuerberater
chèque	Scheck
Code Civil	Bürgerliches Gesetzbuch
Code de Commerce	Handelsgesetzbuch
société; compagnie (more general word)	Gesellschaft
consolidé	konsolidiert
éventuel	eventuell
contrat, convention	Vertrag
conversion (convertible debentures, foreign currencies)	Währungsumrechnung
convertible	Konvertierbar
impôt sur les sociétés	Körperschaftssteuer
coût, prix de revient, prix d'achat (purchase cost)	Anschaffungs- oder Herstellungskosten
comptabilité analytique	Kostenrechnung
frais, charges	Kosten
passif (balance sheet), avoir (bookkeeping), crédit	Passiva (balance sheet), Haben (bookkeeping), Kredit (loan)
créancier, créditeur	Gläubiger, Verbindlichkeit (liability; as used in accounts)
devise	Währung
actif circulant	Umlaufvermögen
valeur actuelle	Buchwert
dettes à court terme	kurzfristige Verbindlichkeiten

161

ENGLISH	SPANISH

D

debenture	obligaciones
debit	debe (bookkeeping), cargo (balance sheet)
debt	deuda
debtor	deudor
deductible	deducible
deferred charge, deferred credit	gasto aplazar
deferred tax provision	tasación diferida
depreciation	depreciación, amortización (provision)
director	consejero vocal
direct overheads	gastos generales directos
discount	descuento
disposal (fixed assets)	disposición
distribution (dividend)	reparto
dividend	dividendo activo
doubtful debts	deudores morosos, saldos dudosos

E

employee	empleados, personal
exchange (foreign)	cambio
exchange rate	tipo de cambio
expenditure, expenses	gasto
exports	exportaciones

F

factory	fábrica
figure	cifra
finished goods	productos terminados
fixed assets	activo fijo, inmovilizado

FRENCH	GERMAN
obligation	Schuldverschreibung, Anleihe
doit, débit (bookkeeping), actif (balance sheet)	Soll (bookkeeping), Aktiva (balance sheet)
créance (not *dette* = liability)	Verbindlichkeit
débiteur	Schuldner
déductible	abzugsfähig
charges à répartir	Rechnungsabgrenzungsposten
provision pour impôt différé	Rückstellung für latente Steuern
amortissements (provision), dotation aux comptes d'amortissements (charge)	Abschreibung
administrateur	Mitglied des Vorstands (des Aufsichtsrats)
frais généraux directement imputables	direkte Gemeinkosten
descompte (bills of exchange)	Disagio (on debentures etc), Skonto (on invoices)
sortie de l'actif, cession	Abgang (fixed assets), Veräusserung
répartition	Ausschüttung
dividende	Dividende
créances douteuses	zweifelhafte Forderungen
salarié exceptionnel	Mitarbeiter ausserordentlich
change	Tausch
taux de change	Kurs
charges, dépenses	Aufwendung, Aufwand
exportations	Ausfuhr, Export
usine	Fabrik
chiffre	Zahl, Betrag
produits finis	Fertigerzeugnisse
immobilisations	Sachanlagen

163

ENGLISH	SPANISH
fixtures and fittings	mobiliaro y enseres
furniture	mobili

G

goods	bienes, mercancias, productos
goodwill	fondo de comercio
gross	bruto
group	grupo
guarantee	garantía

H

hire	alquilar
hire purchase	compra a plazos
holding company	compañia tenedora

I

income	ingreso, renta
income tax	impuesto sobre la renta
indirect costs	costes indirectos
insurance	seguro
intangibles	activo intangible
interest	interés
interim dividend	dividendo provisional
interim report	extracto financiero provisional
investments	immovilizado financiero (securities)
investments in subsidiary and associated companies	participación
invoice	factura
issued (capital)	capital emitido

FRENCH	GERMAN
agencements, aménagements, installations	Betriebs- und Geschäftsausstattung
mobilier, meubles	Einrichtungsgegenstände
marchandises	Waren
fonds de commerce, (on consolidation), survaleur	Firmenwert, Geschäftswert (on consolidation)
brut	brutto
groupe	Konzern
garantie (eg for goods sold), caution (eg for third party's debts)	Bürgschaft (for debts), Gewährleistung (for goods sold)
louer	Miete
location-vente	Kietkauf
société mère	Muttergesellschaft
revenu	Einkommen
impôt sur le bénéfice	Einkommensteuer
frais indirects, frais généraux	indirekte Kosten
assurance	Versicherung
immobilisations incorporelles	immaterielle Wirtschaftgüter
intérêts	Zins; Anteil (ie share in)
acompts sur dividendes	Vorabdividende
rapport intérimaire	Zwischenbericht
investissements (eg in fixed assets)	Investitionen (in fixed assets etc), Finanzanlagen (in balance sheet), Wertpapier (in other securities)
titres de participation	Beteiligung
facture	Rechnung
émis	gezeichnetes Kapital

ENGLISH	SPANISH
L	
land	terrenos
law	ley
lease, leasehold	alquilar, arrendamiento
liabilities	deudas (creditors), pasivo (balance sheet)
limited company	sociedad anónima (SA) (public), sociedad limitada (SL) (private)
limited partnership (with share certificates)	sociedad en commandita
liquidity	liquidez
loans	empréstitos, préstamos
loan capital	capital a préstamo
long term	a largo plazo
loss	pérdida
M	
machinery	maquinaria
manager	gerente
market value	valor mercado
merger	fusión
minorities	participación de la minoria
minutes	actas
money	moneda, dinero
mortgage	hipoteca
motor vehicles	vehiculos

FRENCH	GERMAN
terrains	Grundstück
loi	Gesetz
bail, crédit-bail (leasing agreement)	Erbbaurecht (land and buildings), Leasingvertrag (equipment)
dettes	Verbindlichkeit (creditors), Passiva (balance sheet)
société anonyme (public), société à responsabilité limitée (private)	Aktiengesellschaft (public), Gesellschaft mit beschränkter Haftung (private)
société en commandite (par actions)	Kommanditgesellschaft (auf Aktien)
liquidité	Liquidät
emprunt (payable), prêt (receivable)	Anleihe (payable), Ausleihung (receivable), Kredit
emprunt à long terme	Fremdkapital
à long terme	langfristig
perte	Verlust, Jahresfehlbetrag (for the year), Bilanzverlust (after reserve transfer)
machines, matériel	Maschinen
gérant (SARL); directeur (SA—ie not on board)	Direktor, Geschäftsführer (GmbH)
au cours du marché, au cours du jour	Markwert, Zeitwert
fusion	Verschmelzung
intérêts minoritaires	Ausgleichsposten für Anteile im Fremdbesitz, konzernfremde Gesellschafter
procès-verbal	Protokoll
argent	Geld
hypothèque	Hypothek, Grundpfandrecht
matériel de transport	Kraftfahrzeuge

ENGLISH	SPANISH
N	
net	neto
nominal	nominal
notes to the accounts	anexo al balance, comentarios al balance
O	
office	oficina
ordinary share	acciones ordinarias
overheads	gastos generales
P	
paid up, fully paid	desembolsado
par	nominal
partnership	sociedad en comandita, sociedad comanditaria
patent	patente
pay, payable, paid	paga, a pagar
pension	pensión
pension fund	fondo de pensión
p/e ratio	proporciòn precio-ingresos
personnel	personal
plant	instalaciòn
preference shares	acciones preferentes
premium	prima
prepayments	pagos andelantados
price	precio
prior period	ejercicio anterior
private company	compañia privada de responsibilidad limitada
profit	beneficio, ganancia, utilidades

FRENCH	GERMAN
net	netto
nominal	Nennbetrag
annexe	Ammerkungen, Erläuterungen
bureau	Büro
action	Stammaktie
frais, frais généraux	Gemeinkosten
entièrement libéré	bezahlt, voll eingezahlt
nominale	pari
société en nom collectif	offene Handelsgesellschaft (OHG)
brevet	Patent
payer, à payer, payé	zahlen, zahlbar, bezahlt
pension	Pension, Altersversorgung
caisse de retraite	Pensionskasse
rapport cours/bénéfice	Kurs/Gewinn Verhältnis
personnel, effectif	Belegschaft
matériel	Maschinen
actions préférentielles	Vorzugsaktien
prime	Agio, Aufgeld
compte de régularisation actif, avance (on order etc)	geleistete Anzahlungen (down payments), Rechnungsabgrenzungsposten
prix	Kurs, Preis
exercise antérieur	Vorjahr
société à responsabilité limitée (SARL)	Gesellschaft mit beschränkter Haftung
bénéfice, profit	Gewinn, Jahresüberschuss (for the year), Bilanzgewinn (after reserve transfers)

ENGLISH	SPANISH
profitability	rentabilidad
profit and loss account	cuenta de pérdidas y ganancias
production	producción
provision	provisión
proxy	procuraciòn
public company	azienda pubblica
purchase	acquisto

Q

quoted	cotizada en bolsa

R

rate	tasa, tipo
raw materials	materias primas
receipt	recibo
redemption	reembolso
registered office	domicilio social, sede social
registered (share)	acción nominativa
remuneration	remuneración
rent out, let	alquilar
replacement, replacement value	reposición
report	informe
report and accounts	memoria anual
research and development	investigaciones y desarrollo
reserve	reservas
results	resultados
revaluation	revalorizaciòn
revenue	ingresos, rédito
royalty	derechos

FRENCH	GERMAN
rentabilité	Rentabilität
compte de résultat	Gewinn- und Verlustrechnung
production, fabrication	Herstellung, Produktion
provision	Rückstellung
formule de procuration	Stellvertreter, Vollmacht
société anonyme (SA)	Aktiengesellschaft
acheter (verb), achats de matières et marchandises (noun)	kaufen, einkaufen
admis à la côte officielle d'une bourse de valeurs	am einer Börse notiert
taux	Zinssatz (interest rate), Kurs (quotation, exchange rate)
matières premières	Rohstoffe
quittance (piece of paper), recette	Einnahme (income), Quittung (upon payment)
remboursement	Tilgung
siège social	Sitz
action nominative	Namensaktie
rémunération	Vergütung
donner en location	Vermieten
coût de remplacement	Wiederherstellungswert
rapport	Bericht
plaquette annuelle, rapport annuel	Geschäftsbericht
recherche et développement	Forschung und Entwicklung
réserve	Rücklage (declared), Reserve (secret)
résultats	Ergebnis
réévaluation	Zuschreibung
revenu, produits	Ertrag, Einkommen, Einkünfte
redevance	Lizenzgebühr

171

ENGLISH	SPANISH
S	
salary	sueldo
sale, sell	ventas
security	títulos — valores, valores mobiliarios
share	acción, participación
share capital	capital social
shareholder	accionista
share premium	prima de emisión
shop	tienda
short term	a corto plazo
solvency	solvencia
source and application of funds	origen y aplicación de fondos
stocks (inventories)	existencias, stock
stock exchange	bolsa de comercio
straight line (depreciation)	de línea recta
subsidiary	filial, subsidiaria
sundry	varios
T	
takeover	oferta de adquisición
tax	impuesto
tools	herramientas, utillaje
trade mark	marca
trade union	sindicato

FRENCH	GERMAN
salarie	Gehälter
vente, vendre	Umsatzerlöse, verkaufen
sûreté (on loan), valeur mobilière (shares)	Sicherheit (re loans), Wertpapier (shares, bonds etc)
action (SA), part (SARL, partnership)	Aktie (AG); Anteil (GmbH)
capital social	Grundkapital (AG), Stammkapital (GmbH)
actionnaire	Aktionär (AG), Gesellschafter (GmbH)
prime d'émission (paid for in cash), prime de fusion (on merger), prime d'apport (paid for in assets)	Agio, Kapitalzuzahlung
magasin	Laden
court terme	kurzfristig
solvabilité	Zahlungsfähigkeit
ressources et emplois des fonds, tableau de financement (statement)	Kapitalflussrechnung, Bewegungsbilanz (balance sheet differences)
stocks, valeurs d'exploitation	Vorräte
bourse	Börse
linéaire	linear
filiale	Tochtergesellschaft, anhängiges Unternehmen, Beteiligung
autres, divers	sonstige, verschiedene
offre publique d'achat (cash), offre publique d'éxchange (securities)	Erwerb durch Aktienübernahme
impôt, taxe	Steuer
outilage	Werkseuge
brevet	Warenzeichen
syndicat	Gewerkschaft

ENGLISH	SPANISH
translations (currency)	conversiòn
turnover	ventas

U

unquoted	no cotizado

V

valuation	valoración
value	valor
value added tax (VAT)	impuesto sobre el valor añadido (IVA)
variable	variables
variance	variaciòn

W

wages	salarios
working capital	capital circulante
work in progress	productos en curso

Y

yield	rendabilidad

FRENCH	GERMAN
conversion	Umrechnung
chiffre d'affaires, ventes	Umsatz
non admis á la côte officielle d'une bourse de valeurs	nicht notiert
évaluation	Bewertung
valeur	Wert
taxe sur la valeur ajoutée (TVA)	Mehrwertsteuer, Umsatzsteuer
variable	leistungstabhängig
écart	Abweichung
salaires	Löhne
fonds de roulement	Betriebsmittel
produits ou travaux en cours	unfertige Erzeugnisse
rendement	Rendite

Index